Labradoodles

Joan Hustace Walker

BARRON'S

Contents

What Is the Labradoodle?

On the surface, the answer to "What is the
Labradoodle?" seems simple. He's a LABRADor mixed
with a pOODLE, or a "Labradoodle," right? Yes . . .
and no. The term "Labradoodle" is often used for a
variety of iterations of the Labradoodle/Poodle cross.

In the strictest sense of the word, "Labradoodle" refers to the simple, straight, one-time cross between any Labrador Retriever and any Poodle. The Australian Labradoodle, or AL, is different in that it not only has multiple generations (often 16 or more!) of Australian Labradoodle/Australian Labradoodle in his lineage, but he also has infusions of other purebreds in the early generations, to create what is known as the "Australian Labradoodle."

But, there are also early generation Labradoodles, Labradoodle crossbacks (a Labradoodle bred back to either a Labrador Retriever or a Poodle), and multigenerational Labradoodles. And all of these iterations—from the Labradoodle to the Australian Labradoodle—have unique and distinct qualities.

To understand more about how the Labradoodle, Australian Labradoodle, and everything in between came into being, it is necessary to cross the Pacific Ocean and learn about the Labradoodle's origins in Australia.

WORKING ORIGINS OF A DESIGNER BREED

The Labradoodle began as a solution to a problem. In the early 1980s, the puppy-breeding manager for the Royal Guide Dog Association of Australia, Wally Conron, received a challenging request.

A vision-impaired woman from Hawaii wrote to the guide dog association, inquiring if an allergy-free guide dog could be had from the center. She was not allergic to dogs, but her husband was, and in order to have a guide dog in the home without her husband suffering, she had to find a guide dog that her husband wasn't allergic to.

The guide dog's puppy program bred only Labradors. However, Conron thought he had a solution to the problem: train Standard Poodles as service dogs. He reasoned that Poodles had a non-shedding coat, were often not a problem for people with allergies to dogs, and the Standard Poodle, which could be up to 27 inches (69 cm) tall at the shoulder, would be sizeable enough for a working service dog.

Problem solved! Or so he thought . . . ". . . after rejecting countless Poodles with various problems, some two years and 33 disappointing trials later, I still hadn't found an appropriate dog for the job," writes Conron in an article he penned in the July 10, 2007 issue of *Reader's Digest*. "In desperation, I decided to cross a Standard Poodle with one of our best-producing Labradors."

That initial crossing produced three puppies. Coat and saliva samples were sent to the couple to determine if any of the puppies would prove to be allergy-free. One puppy's samples were successful. "Sultan" would become the first hypoallergenic service dog. Before that would be possible, however, Conron was faced with a rather desperate situation: No one wanted to be a puppy raiser—the early training and socialization aspect that is so important to the success of service dogs—for Sultan and his littermates. Even though the guide dog association, with which Conron was associated, had a three to six month waiting list of people wanting to be puppy raisers, no one wanted a "mixed breed" puppy to raise.

The First Doodle

According to the Australian Labradoodle's foundation club in Australia (the Australian Labradoodle Association [ALA]), a white Standard Poodle imported from Sweden was used in Conron's initial breeding of Labrador to Standard Poodle.

Eight weeks after the pups had been born, Conron still hadn't found puppy-raising homes for them. Largely out of frustration and annoyance, Conron stopped referring to the puppies as crossbred, and instead coined the name "Labradoodle" to describe the allergy-free guide dog puppies that he had worked so hard to breed and had been carefully rearing.

The new name worked. In a matter of weeks, the pups not only found puppy-raising homes, but news of the "new" allergy-free breed reached other guide dog associations, as well as those who wanted an allergy-free dog as a pet.

Over time, Labradoodle Sultan finished his vision-impaired service dog training and was ready to be delivered to his new owner and her dog-allergic husband in Hawaii. The arrival of Sultan in Hawaii received much press, made international news, and fueled the desire for the Labradoodle not only as a service dog but also as the answer to many dog-loving people who sought a hypoallergenic dog.

Conron's Labrador/Poodle cross was a hit, so Conron set out to breed more to be used as service dogs.

In an attempt to find the healthiest Standard Poodles with the most suitable attributes and characteristics to breed with the guide dog program's Labradors, Conron approached the Kennel Control Council of Australia. However, the response Conron received was anything but warm: The KCC reportedly warned its members that they would be banned from dog shows and litter registrations for life if any of their dogs participated in Conron's program.

The next litter Conron bred of Labradoodles produced ten puppies. Only three proved to be allergy-free to humans. It was at this time that Conron became acutely concerned that he may have created a huge demand for a hypoallergenic dog that could not be produced with any consistency.

Additionally, Conron worried that backyard breeders would pick up on the craze for the Labradoodle—that they would breed for profit alone, with no

Do You Have a Dog Allergy?

The National Institutes of Health says that detectable levels of pet dander are in every home in the U.S. That statistic includes homes that don't have dogs! And, if you are one of the approximately 65 percent of American households that have a pet (American Pet Products Association 2015 estimate), your dog's dander is everywhere—including places where your dog has never set paw.

But, how do you know if you are truly allergic to dogs or if it is something else? According to the American College of Allergies, Asthma, and Immunology (ACAAI), "If your nose runs or you start sneezing and wheezing after petting or playing with a dog, you may be allergic to dogs." The symptoms are the same as any other nasal allergy, and according to the ACAAI include:

- Sneezing or a runny or stuffy nose
- Facial pain (from nasal congestion)
- Coughing, chest tightness, shortness of breath, and wheezing
- Watery, red, or itchy eyes
- Skin rash or hives

Dogs produce multiple allergens, or proteins that can cause allergies. These allergens are found in dog hair, dander, saliva, and urine. All dogs produce allergens, and according to the ACAAI, studies have not shown that any breed or coat type—or dog, for that matter—can be truly hypoallergenic (i.e., not cause allergic reactions).

But, it could also be something else: Dust and pollen in a dog's coat can also cause allergy symptoms, according to the ACAAI. And the less a dog is bathed, and the longer or more coat the dog has, the more likely it is that the dog can serve as a "sponge" for dust and pollen, both inside and outdoors. In those cases, the allergy is to dust or pollen, not to the dog. Bathing the dog at least once a week and utilizing other strategies to minimize dust and pollen (i.e., run high-efficiency particulate air [HEPA] cleaners continuously in the bedroom or living room to reduce allergens, use a high-efficiency vacuum cleaner or a central vacuum to reduce allergen levels, etc.) can help.

concern for the hereditary qualities of the sire and dam or their inability to predict or produce a low-allergen, non-shedding puppy.

DOODLE MANIA

Doodle Mania—everything and anything bred to the poodle—was in full swing by the late 1980s. Breeders were popping up overnight, with virtually anyone who could mate a Poodle with a Labrador getting into the business of puppy selling. Confusion ensued when consumers purchased a Labradoodle puppy, and it was not what they expected or were told it would be. Puppies grew to be large dogs with shedding coats, high activity levels, and sometimes unstable temperaments—the latter of which happens anytime a dog is bred by those more interested in financial gain than the health and welfare of the animals involved.

Amid all this confusion, however, there were breeders who were already looking to develop a purebred from this early hybrid that would combine all the great qualities of the Labrador and Poodle, as well as develop a low-shedding coat. What these breeders were working on was what would become known as the "Australian Labradoodle."

LABRADOODLES TO AUSTRALIAN LABRADOODLES (AND EVERYTHING IN BETWEEN)

Navigating the world of Labradoodles is much like trying to read a dissertation in biology: F1, F1B, F2, multigenerational, early generation, purebred? If you're confused, you're not alone. Understanding the nomenclature used to describe each dog

in a Labradoodle or AL pedigree is important though, as it determines what you are getting as a puppy—from temperament and coat type to breed characteristics. The letters and numbers represent the actual percentages of breeds involved in the making of your pup. The following is a brief look at what breeders offer and what the Labradoodle "alphabet soup" of Fs and numbers represents.

Labradoodles (F1)

The Labradoodle, or F1 (first generation of Labrador/Poodle cross), is a simple cross of any Labrador Retriever with any Poodle. The Poodle is most commonly a Standard Poodle, but it can be a Miniature Poodle or even a Toy Poodle.

As a first-generation breeding, the Labradoodle (F1) litter can have wide variations among the puppies in not only sizes but also coat types, temperaments, and drives.

The Cockapoo

The first Poodle cross was reportedly the Cockapoo, a Cocker Spaniel/Poodle mix that was quite popular in the 1950s.

What's the F?

The "F" in biological terms stands for "filial," or the generation after the parental generation. When the nomenclature F1 is used in describing hybrid dog breeds (hybrid meaning two distinctly different dog breeds), it represents the distance from the first crossing of the distinctly different parental types.

Hypoallergenic Dogs: Do They Exist?

According to a 2008 study, even though 62 percent of American households have pets, only five percent of dog owners were skin-prick-test positive to dog allergens. The 2012 study "Do Hypoallergenic Cats and Dogs Exist?" (from the Division of Allergy & Immunology at the University of South Florida and the James A. Haley Veterans' Hospital, Tampa, Florida) found that the source of allergens from dogs is *not* from the dog's dander or from his hair, as many breeders of "hypoallergenic" dogs would like the general public to believe. Rather, the allergens are from the dog's tongue and parotid glands, with reservoirs of the allergens found in the dog's saliva, dander, and fur. In homes, the 2012 study noted that areas with the highest concentrations of allergens were in bedding, upholstery furniture, and carpeting.

Per the 2012 study, "Many misconceptions persist among physicians, health care professionals, and the general population about pet dander allergy," when the allergens are really coming from the dog's saliva and parotid glands. So no matter how low-shed, no shed, reduced dander forming, etc., a dog or breed is, nothing really matters except for the allergens contained in the dog's saliva.

What's the bottom line? A truly hypoallergenic dog does not exist. Though you may find a particular dog's saliva to contain less of the allergen that triggers your sensitivities, and a dog with far less reservoirs for the allergen to accumulate (i.e., very little dander, low shedding, less drooling), there are still no guarantees.

Sizes of the F1 Typically, the Labradoodle (F1) litter produces large to very large Labradoodles (as tall as 27 inches [69 cm] at the shoulder or taller). If the Labrador female was bred to a smaller sized Poodle, such as a Miniature or Toy Poodle, the litter will not be all small. It will be a variety of sizes from large to smaller.

Coat types of the F1 The first generation of Labrador/Poodle cross creates a wide range of coat types, from those with hair like the Labrador Retriever to those with longer hair that is straight, wavy, or even wiry in appearance. The F1's coat can have an undercoat (as with the Labrador) and it can shed, and shed profusely. The first-generation litter also may have pups with a Poodle-type coat—a denser, tightly curled, woolly coat that is less likely to shed. And, there may be pups with somewhere in between a hair and a wool coat. Note: None of the F1 Labradoodles will have the soft, low-shed fleece or wool coat that is distinctive of the Australian Labradoodle (more on this later).

Colors and Patterns in the F1 In the first generation Labrador/Poodle, colors will

Hybrid Vigor Not So Vigorous?

Mixed-breed dogs have long been thought of as possessing the genetics to be healthier than either purebred parent. But, is this true? Supporters of mixed breeds, including breeders of all the "poo" crosses, have long held that the results (puppies) from first generation mixes (purebred breed "1" crossed with purebred breed "2" were much healthier than either of the breeds used to produce the hybrid.

According to a 2013 study from the University of California, Davis (UC Davis) and published in the June 1, 2013 issue of the *Journal of the American Veterinary Medical Association*, the validity of "hybrid vigor" is in serious jeopardy. The study reviewed 90,000 medical records of dogs from 1995 to 2010 that had been seen at UC Davis' School of Veterinary Medicine. Researchers found that mixed-breed dogs were equally as susceptible as purebred dogs to 13 heritable medical conditions, which included hip dysplasia, hypoadrenocorticism and hyperadrenocorticism, cancers, lens luxation, and patellar luxation. Additionally, mixed breeds were at higher risk to suffer from ruptured cranial cruciate ligaments (a ligament in the dog's "knee") than purebreds.

"The public is under the impression that mixed breeds exhibit vigor and will not express genetic disorders. This simply is not true," said Anita M. Oberbauer, Ph.D., professor, department chair of the department of animal sciences at UC Davis, animal physiologist, and the study's lead author (November 7, 2013 interview, VIN News Service).

The study determined that the prevalence of genetic disorders in both mixed breed and purebred dog populations was related to the specific disorder. The study concluded that "recently derived breeds or those from similar lineages appeared to be more susceptible to certain disorders that affect all closely related purebred dogs, whereas disorders with equal prevalence in the two populations suggested that those disorders represented more ancient mutations that are widespread through the dog population."

vary and will depend on the color genetics possessed by the parents. Generally speaking, the F1 Labradoodle will have less variability in his coat colors and patterns than later generations, as the infusion of Poodle is responsible for the multitude of colors and markings that appear in later generations of Labradoodles.

Temperaments of the F1 A dog's temperament is a combination of inherited characteristics and the environment in which the puppy is raised. As for the inherited portion of the dog's temperament, with the F1, if a sociable, sweet Labrador Retriever is bred to an equally as friendly and calm Standard Poodle, the puppies will most likely take after

The American Labradoodle

This term is sometimes used to describe a Labradoodle and any of its variations, such as the F2, F1B, Fn, and early generation.

their parents and will be friendly, intelligent, active, and easily trained. Temperament problems occur, though, when a poor temperament (e.g., fearful, reactive, dominant, aggressive, etc.) is introduced genetically by either or both parents. Environment influences the ability of a puppy to reach his full genetic potential—whether that potential is for a poor temperament or a stellar temperament. In other words, how the puppy is raised while at the breeder's home (and afterward) can greatly influence whether a puppy with the genetics to become a fantastically gregarious fellow actually develops into the friendly Labradoodle he was born to be or, conversely, develops into a fearful one. Likewise, the environment at the breeder's home can confirm that a naturally fearful and reactive puppy becomes fearful and reactive—or that inroads are already being made to help the environment suppress genetics and assist the naturally shy puppy to become much friendlier.

Activity Level of the F1 A defining characteristic of the F1 Labradoodle is that he is frequently a high-drive, very high activity level dog. F1s require a lot of exercise, not only as long, fast-paced walks, but also as high-energy, all-out daily runs. A large, fenced

Did You Know?

Colors and patterns can be determined through DNA testing, and breeders sometimes use this testing to help make breeding decisions if the litter colors and markings are of importance.

yard is a must as is the ability of the owner to take the doodle to the dog park to enjoy romps with other Labradoodles.

F1B, F2, Fn, Early Generation and Multigenerational

F1B The F1B nomenclature designates an F1 Labradoodle (Labrador/Poodle) crossed back (the "B" part of the nomenclature) with a purebred—either Labrador or Poodle.

Do Non-shedding Coats Shed?

The term "non-shedding" coat is not entirely correct, because all dogs' coats shed. Coats that are very curly or tightly woven tend to grow longer before they shed. When the hairs do shed, because of the density of the coat or the curl and/or wave, the shed hair gets caught in the live hair and must be brushed out to prevent mats and tangles. The highly desirable fleece and woolly coats found in the Australian Labradoodle may not cause hairs to be swept up from the floor and furniture; however, the dog will require constant brushing. Left unbrushed, the dog's shed hairs will cause dense mats that, when left alone, will require a full body shaving of the dog.

In order to gain more non-shedding coats and less skin dander, this cross is typically back to a purebred Poodle. The F1B Labradoodle is almost always, therefore, three-quarters Poodle and one-quarter

Double Doodles/ North American Retriever

This term describes a Labradoodle/ Goldendoodle cross, which is one-quarter Golden Retriever, one-quarter Labrador, and one-half Poodle.

Aren't All Purebreds Registered with the American Kennel Club (AKC)?

Yes and no. To be able to compete in AKC conformation events (where intact dogs are judged on their build, coat, and movement) a dog must be registered with the AKC as a purebred. Dogs with disqualifying faults, as well as debilitating health problems and/or hereditary diseases, poor temperaments, and questionable parentage, may be registered. (DNA testing is not required at the current time for most dogs being shown, so there is no way to ensure that a dog is actually who is registered as a purebred with the club.) The AKC maintains the registry and keeps it open to anyone who wants to pay to register their dogs.

Some breed clubs, however, prefer to maintain their own registries and don't want to turn over their registries to the AKC. Why? Because when the individual breed club maintains the registry, the breed club can dictate what health, conformation, and temperament tests a dog must have passed to be registered as a purebred with the club.

The Jack Russell Terrier Club of America (JRTCA), for example, went through an agonizing period in the 1980s when members of the breed club wanted to seek out AKC recognition. To become recognized by the AKC would mean turning over their registry and their control of the breed. The club actually had a split in its membership, with a group of members forming a new club so that it could receive AKC recognition.

The AL breed clubs have members, too, who would like to seek AKC recognition. The Australian Labradoodle (NOT the Labradoodle, which is a designer dog or mix) has been bred for enough generations as a purebred to begin the steps to seek AKC recognition. However, a strong portion of clubs don't want to give up control of the registry and required health tests.

Where the club will go in the next decade is uncertain, but, for now, the AL is not recognized as a purebred by the AKC. Both breed clubs maintain their own registries and their own qualifications for registration.

Labrador. F1B litters generally contain more puppies with non-shedding, low-dander coats and a higher possibility for pups that have Poodle-like woolly coats. Some breeders breed only F1B Labradoodles.

F2 Labradoodle The F2 nomenclature refers to the second generation Labradoodle—the breeding of a Labradoodle to another Labradoodle. A second generation is still half Labrador and half Poodle and does not have enough generations yet to start producing a specific breed type. Some breeders report that the F2 generations have less non-shedding, low or no dander coats than the F1 generation. Because of this, some breeders have chosen to focus on F1B Labradoodles.

Fn Labradoodle This nomenclature represents any number of generations for Labradoodle/Labradoodle, with the variation of the "n" determining what generation the individual dog is. But, here's where things get a little complicated. The "n" for any cross between Labradoodles becomes a +1 to the lowest "n" factor. For example, an F1 bred to an F3 will produce a litter of F2s.

Early Gens This refers to the early generations of Labradoodle breeding, such as the F1, F2, and F1B types.

Multigenerational Labradoodles As noted above, after three generations of breeding Labradoodle to Labradoodle, the offspring of two F3 parents and beyond are referred to as multigen, or multigenerational.

Australian Labradoodles

The Australian Labradoodle, or AL, is a purebred dog breed that has been bred for generations to produce a dog with consistent temperaments, conformation, sizes, and coat types. The early generations of the AL included Labradors, Poodles, Labradoodles, F1Bs, and multigens, as well as infusions of five different breeds: the Irish Water Spaniel, the Curly-Coated Retriever, the American Cocker Spaniel, the English Cocker Spaniel, and the Soft-Coated Wheaten Terrier. Infusions are no longer allowed in the American Labradoodle Club of America (ALCA); infusions are allowed in certain restricted circumstances within a breeder's program in the American Labradoodle Association of America (ALAA). Most ALs have Australian Labradoodle/Australian Labradoodle for up to 16 or more generations.

The Australian Labradoodle comes in three sizes: standard, medium, and miniature. Breed standards from the ALA, ALAA, and ALCA all call for the following distinctions in sizes, with measurements taken from the shoulder to the floor:

- Standard ALs are 21–24 inches (53–61 cm) but not over 25 inches (63.5 cm) at the shoulder, with 21–23 inches (53–58 cm) as ideal for females and 22–24 inches (56–61 cm) at the shoulders as ideal for males.
- Medium ALs are 17–20 inches (43–51 cm) but not over 21 inches (53 cm) at the shoulder, with females ideally 17–19 inches (43–48 cm) and males ideally 18–20 inches (46–51 cm).
- Miniature ALs are 14–16 inches (36–41 cm) but not over 17 inches (43 cm), and there is no size differentiation between males and females.

The Australian Labradoodle possesses a low-shedding fleece or wool coat. Both coat types require brushing to remove the shed hair from the coat to prevent mats. The AL fleece coat is generally light, silky, soft, and free flowing. It can be nearly straight, loosely waved, or have a very definite wave, too. The AL wool coat ranges from tightly woven curls to the more preferable loose, hollow spiral curls.

Australian Labradoodle Colors and Patterns

Black pigmented colors require that the AL's nose, eye rims, and lips should all be black, and the eyes should be a very dark brown. Colors include: Chalk, Cream, Apricot, Gold, Red, Black, Blue, and Silver.

Liver pigmented colors require that the AL have chocolate colored noses, eye rims, and lips and allow for a lighter colored eye. Eyes may be dark amber to pale hazel-green eyes. Coat colors include: Caramel Ice, Caramel Cream, Caramel, Caramel Red, Chocolate, Lavender, Café, and Parchment.

Coat Patterns

A "solid" coat is one color (either black or liver pigment colors) and preferably has no white markings. The Australian Labradoodle allows for a small white flash on the chest, feet, or tail (not to exceed 2.5 cm in diameter).

"Solid with white markings" is a coat pattern that allows for small white spots or patches on the chest, toes, and/or tip of the tail.

"Abstract" is a coat pattern that is predominately one of the colors listed under black

and liver pigmented coat colors and white, with white making up less than 50 percent of the dog's entire coat.

A "parti" colored coat is 50 percent or more of white, with spots/patches of any other solid color. Symmetrical markings are preferred; freckling of the coat's solid color (also referred to as "ticking") in the white areas of the coat is not encouraged but is acceptable.

"Phantom" coat patterns are similar to what you would see on a Rottweiler or Doberman, for example. The primary body color is solid with the second color appearing as markings above the eyes, on the sides of the muzzle, on the cheeks, and on the underside of the ears. Also, the markings appear throat to forechest, or in a chin and forechest pattern. Markings appear also under the tail, on the feet, and up the legs.

"Sable" coat patterns consist of a body color of any of the listed colors, with black-tipped hairs.

"Brindle" is a characteristic tiger-stripe pattern that is a layering of black hairs over a lighter color. Brindling is easiest to detect when the puppy's coat is still short and smooth. Once the coat grows out, it can be harder to see the coat color pattern.

The "multi" coat pattern is the almost "anything goes" category, in which multiple colors or patterns can be seen. Examples include a phantom pattern with a large white marking or a parti-color dog with the colored patches being sable or brindle.

Breed Clubs for the Australian Labradoodle

Labradoodle Association of Australia (LAA): This was the first known club for the development of the Australian Labradoodle as a breed. It began in the late 1990s and wrote the first breed standard for the Australian Labradoodle, but it disbanded due to lack of support. The club was reformed in 2002 as the Australian Labradoodle Association, or ALA.

Australian Labradoodle Association (ALA): The ALA took off where the LAA left off and was founded in Australia in 2002. The ALA continues to work toward the refinement and development of the Australian Labradoodle as a purebred dog.

International Australian Labradoodle Association (IALA): The IALA was incorporated in 2004 in Hawaii and serves as the umbrella organization for the ALA and ALAA. The IALA is focused on the following:

- Establish and verify pedigrees for Australian Labradoodle blood lines
- Provide ancestry of registered lines completely transparent to the public (no hidden in-breeding or additional infused breeds)
- Refocus the efforts of breeders on the health testing of previously untested lines
- Promote Australian Labradoodle-to-Australian Labradoodle breeding with consistent results
- Introduce new Labrador-to-Poodle-only lines to widen the gene pool of top quality Labradoodles

Australian Labradoodle Association of America (ALAA): Founded in 2005 in the United States, the ALAA is a sister organization to the ALA and falls under the umbrella leadership of the International Australian Labradoodle Association (IALA). The ALAA requires DNA testing of all breeding dogs, as well as a minimum of health and genetic testing to be performed. In addition, the ALAA worked with Pawprints Genetics to develop a genetic testing panel for the Australian Labradoodle, and based on the level of testing

a breeder performs the breeder is awarded a "silver" or "gold" paw certification.

Australian Labradoodle Club of America (ALCA): Founded in 2004, the ALCA is based on the breeding lines of two former Australian Labradoodle breeders from Australia, and the registry is limited to these specific lines of Australian Labradoodles. The ALCA does not allow for infusions under any circumstances; however, the ALCA does not require or maintain an extensive online database to health records and test results for their registered dogs.

*Note: Many Australian Labradoodle breeders can be and are members of both clubs.

The Australian & International Australian Cobberdog Club (AIACC): Founded in 2012, it, too, is a club made of breeders of Australian Labradoodles. However, the AIACC breed club states that the Australian Cobberdog is "the genuine, non-corrupted Australian Labradoodle."

Popular "Doodle" Mixes

Goldendoodle (Golden Retriever/Poodle)
Schnoodle (Miniature Schnauzer/Poodle)
Cavoodle (Cavalier King Charles Spaniel/Poodle)
Roodle (Rottweiler/Poodle)
Yorkiepoo (Yorkshire Terrier/Poodle)
Shihpoo (Shih Tzu/Poodle)
Maltipoo (Maltese/Poodle)
Poochon (Bichon Frise/Poodle)
Lhasapoo (Lhasa Apso/Poodle)

Characteristics of
the Labradoodle

Labradoodles are intelligent, high-energy,
athletic dogs who have an affinity for
water, people, and therapy work.

The Labradoodle created nothing short of an international sensation when the first guide dog was delivered to Hawaii in the late 1980s. Since then, the Labradoodle has been touted as the most popular crossbred dog in North America, and has far surpassed any of the other Poodle crosses.

However, from claims of hypoallergenic coats to being the perfect dog for all families, hype and hyperbole surrounding the Labradoodle are difficult to separate from fact. The differences between the Labradoodle (F1), the Australian Labradoodle, and everything in between are fairly significant, further making the decision as to whether the Labradoodle is the best dog for you more confusing. Often, puppy owners think they are getting one type of dog, but what they receive is completely different.

The following is a summary of Labradoodle and Australian Labradoodle characteristics that must be considered—both positive characteristics along with those that prove more challenging—before you decide if the Labradoodle or AL is right for you and your lifestyle.

LABRADOODLE/AUSTRALIAN LABRADOODLE QUALITIES

Love of water: The Labradoodle is the product of two water retrieving, hunting breeds. The Australian Labradoodle is derived from no less than five hunting dog breeds that all work well in water. So, a love of water—or at least no fear of getting his paws, coat, and all else wet and/or muddy—is often a common quality. If you enjoy being outdoors, visiting lakes, ponds, bays, and such, the Labradoodle/Australian Labradoodle could very much enjoy these activities with you. Of course, there's no guarantee, as there is always the pup that may want nothing to do with water. And, unfortunately, somehow baths do not apply to the "love of water."

Entertaining: The Labradoodle and Australian Labradoodle get their love of entertaining and uncanny sense of "doggie" humor and ability to learn tricks honestly: Poodles have a very long history (dating back to the

Bailey, The Therapy Dog

On Fridays, the children at the Cohen Children's Hospital in Long Island, New York have something to look forward to: It's the day that Bailey, a 5-year-old, apricot, medium-sized, male Australian Labradoodle, comes to visit.

Bailey, along with his owner and handler, Mike Kroeber, and Mike's wife, Chris, have been visiting the hospital in an official therapy dog role for four years. But, before Bailey could volunteer as a therapy dog at the children's hospital, he had to pass the hospital's test.

"There are usually ten to fifteen dogs being tested at one time. Bailey was one of the three dogs to pass that day, and he was the youngest dog ever to work at the hospital," explains Mike.

Every Friday, Bailey works in the main hospital building, first stopping by to give staff members a much needed "Bailey break" from their day. Then, Bailey drops by the outpatient center to visit in the playrooms, and later makes his way to see the inpatients in their individual rooms.

Bailey knows a variety of tricks: high five, wave hello, balance things on his nose (his record is five cookies!), play dead, spin, walk, dance, and more. Mike shows the children how to get Bailey to do his tricks, which brings a lot of smiles and giggles, and something else, too. Mike explains that the hospitalized children are constantly taking orders from everyone: "They are poked and prodded and told, 'Do this . . . take this.' So, it's nice when they can tell someone else what to do." And, Bailey is happy to do it. Bailey has helped a child, who was refusing to walk, to get out of bed and start dancing with him. Bailey was also invited to one little girl's Make-a-Wish party: The girl wanted to go to Disney World to have tea with princesses. When she fell too ill to make the trip, she changed her wish to tea with princesses *and* Bailey. So, Bailey sat with the princesses and enjoyed the tea party with the little girl. "All I could think of that day was that little girl smiling and having a good time," says Mike.

So, for a few minutes every Friday, Bailey transforms a child who is usually defined by his or her illness, into someone who is just a child playing with a dog. And, at that moment, life is good.

early 18th century) of performing in "troupes" in Europe. Poodles danced, played chess, and did amazing athletic feats—and made it look easy. Learning tricks, making people laugh, and having an honest desire to please and entertain are traits that the Labradoodle and Australian Labradoodle share.

Keenly Intelligent: As the product of two highly intelligent breeds, the Labradoodle probably has more brains than is good for him. (The Australian Labradoodle has even more "brainy" breeds involved in his ancestry.) Unilaterally, if the Labradoodle/Australian Labradoodle is left to his own means, he will come up with creative activities, none of which you will find nearly as entertaining and clever as he does. Both the Labradoodle and Australian Labradoodle need to be mentally stimulated. Fortunately, with a combination of regular training, involvement in sporting events, and copious outdoor exercise (in which he gets to see, smell, and experience new things), the doodle's daily need for quality mental stimulation can be met by most owners.

Trainability: As much of a genius as this dog is, trainability (the ease with which he can be trained), however, is mixed. The F1 Labradoodle can lean more toward his highly sensitive Poodle roots, or he can lean more toward his low-key, easily trained Labrador roots. That is, of course, if the Lab parent is from highly-trainable, well-bred lines. Often, he is not. Today's quality Labrador Retriever breeders do not knowingly allow their lines to be freely "mixed" with a neighbor's Poodle, in which case, the F1 Labradoodle breeder will use what he or she has access to, which could be a classic Lab-type temperament or a Lab that is exceedingly high energy, lacking focus, and possibly even rank-challenging.

The Australian Labradoodle has been bred for generations to have a consistent, keen intelligence that is paired with a more focused, calmer temperament. There are always variations within the breed; however, the AL is recognized and sought after for calmness and high trainability.

Sensitivity: The Labradoodle and the Australian Labradoodle are both exceptionally sensitive to physical and emotional changes in their owners and in people around them. They excel as therapy dogs, emotional support dogs, guide dogs, and service dogs. Without question, the doodle will be a sensitive and a loyal companion.

Activity level: The Labradoodle can, and often does, have an exceptionally high activity level. Many potential puppy owners don't realize just how active these doodles can be. As a young adolescent, the Labradoodle can require up to an hour or more of brisk walking or jogging daily, as well as a once-a-day, all-out, off-leash run in a large, fenced-in area.

The highly active doodle, especially if he is of large size, can be exceptionally challenging for the young family that can't provide the exercise requirements that the F1 cross demands. Full of energy and with no outlet to burn off steam, doodles can knock children over, play roughly, and get even more excited from the children's running and screams. This rough play and excitement can cause injuries. Just as with any other high-energy breed, if the Labradoodle is then banished to a crate or the backyard, his behavior will go from bad to worse. And, usually it's a short trip from the backyard to the local shelter to relinquish the "problem" dog.

Though the Australian Labradoodle is athletic, and is able to perform at high-energy levels, once he has become an adult, the typical AL is content to operate on your activity level; he can be your best snuggle buddy and he can be a great jogging/hiking [fill in your activity here] partner. Can an AL have an exceptionally high activity level and a limited ability to focus? Yes; however, quality Australian Labradoodle breeders are breeding for the calmer, athletic, highly trainable dog.

Athleticism: The Labradoodle and the Australian Labradoodle are true canine athletes. They have speed, jumping ability, and coordination. To put it bluntly, the doodle is made to excel at sports. Whether it's agility, fly ball, dock diving, or disc golf, the doodle outshines most other breeds.

People Lover: For the most part, the doodle is a gregarious, fun-loving, adorable puppy that grows into a boisterous, people-loving dog. Good manners are necessary to learn from the get-go for both the Labradoodle and the Australian Labradoodle, as well as everything in between (see "Training Basics," pages 76–89). If not trained, the loving doodle can become an obnoxious "teen" that at full-size is jumping up on people for attention. Part of the doodle's training requires continuous, good socialization opportunities and exposures to help the puppy grow in his affinity for and comfortableness around people of all ages, sizes, and colors.

Belle of the [Dog] Ball: Labradoodle and Australian Labradoodle owners tend to con-

Life Span

The average Labradoodle and Australian Labradoodle have a life span of 10–14 years, with many healthy ALs living past 14.

gregate at the dog park and even build social groups around their dogs—and for good reason. The doodle comes from dog-friendly lineage, regardless of whether he is a simple cross or an Australian Labradoodle. Of course there are exceptions to every rule, but, in general, doodles are very dog friendly, which is awesome because you will need to have a dog park or outlet to give your Labradoodle/Australian Labradoodle a place to run and play full out, and still be safe.

Good with Children? Yes, but with this caveat, which is true of all dogs and children: As a parent, you must be able to provide constant, close supervision between child and dog. The F1 Labradoodle has one "parent" breed (Lab) that is recognized for being overly patient and tolerant of children. The other parent breed (Poodle) is sensitive, and often more reactive. The Australian Labradoodle is bred to be good with children and adults and is often a therapy dog. However, this does not mean a dog of any age or breed should be expected to tolerate mistreatment from children, whether intended or accidental.

Troubles can ensue when a sensitive doodle is in a home with:
- Excitable children, as this excitement gets the doodle excited, too, and accidents can happen.
- Toddlers, because accidental pokes, tugs, pulls, and falls on top of the doodle may not be tolerated well.
- Children who like to play roughly with a dog are either not tolerated well, or met with even rougher, inappropriate play or defensive reactions.

- A parent who is not willing to supervise or separate children from dogs 24 hours a day, 7 days a week.

After all, a doodle is a dog, and owners must make sure their expectations for the dog are real. Bottom line . . . Parents must provide close and attentive supervision between dogs (including puppies and adolescents) and children at all times.

GROOMING REQUIREMENTS

As far as coat types, they all require time and effort. The hair coat of the Labradoodle is easier to maintain; however, it is a shedding coat that is definitely not hypoallergenic and one that sheds all the time and everywhere. You will spend a large amount of time sweeping your floors and vacuuming your furniture to remove hair.

Professional grooming for a large dog is expensive: well over $60, and even higher in certain areas, for brushing out a *well-kept* dog, ear cleaning, nail trim, bath, haircut, and blow dry. If your doodle isn't in good coat shape, you will pay more—potentially much more—for his grooming session. And, you can expect to go through the grooming cycle at least every month to six weeks (depending on the type of coat, how well you maintain it, and what type of clip you like to keep your Labradoodle in) to as frequently as every two weeks. You will need to budget for this expense.

BIGGER DOG = BIGGER EXPENSES

Speaking of expenses, the larger the dog, the bigger the dog's expenses will be. Crates are priced according to size. Preventive pre-scriptions for fleas, ticks, and heartworm are all dosed and priced according to the size and weight of the dog. Bigger dogs eat more food. The large F1 Labradoodle and the standard Australian Labradoodle will simply cost more than a smaller dog.

IS THE LABRADOODLE HEALTHIER?

A common selling point of any cross-bred dog—and this is not limited to the Labradoodle—is that any cross between two different dog breeds will produce a healthier puppy due to "hybrid vigor." Recent studies have shown the theory of hybrid vigor to be in doubt. (See "Hybrid Vigor Not So Vigorous," page 10.)

Health with the F1 Labradoodle really boils down to the health of the pup's parents, and

Fleece and wool coats require daily brushing to clear the coat of dead hairs that will otherwise produce to-the-skin, dense mats.

Even with the best intentions, owners often find the grooming requirements of a Labradoodle or Australian Labradoodle overwhelming. Owners frequently fall behind on the grooming chores and wind up with a doodle that requires a surgical clip, and the entire matted mess has to be removed at the veterinarian's office or at the groomer's. It's unhealthy and terribly uncomfortable for a dog to become matted, but before you swear you would never allow a dog to be one solid, awful mat, remember that it doesn't take much neglect for a dog's coat to get to this point.

how extensively the breeder has health-tested his or her breeding dogs. Even health testing is not a guarantee of great health, as many hereditary diseases are not fully understood at this time or don't have genetic testing available. With that said, the AL breed clubs have made an effort to determine hereditary diseases in Australian Labradoodles and have required and recommended health testing for all breeding dogs.

Again, the general rule for the F1 Labradoodle, the Australian Labradoodle, and everything in between is that the puppy that comes from generations of healthy stock that have been tested (and certified clear of known, problematic genetic diseases) is much more likely to be healthier than the puppy that comes from untested dogs.

THINKING IT THROUGH

Labradoodles and Australian Labradoodles are touted as the perfect breed, which is a dangerous statement to make because it sets unrealistic expectations for the doodle in the home. Unrealistic expectations lead to the greatest rate of failure among doodle owners. The doodle can't possibly live up to the hype and hyperbole of being the perfect dog—because he is a *dog*. The perfect housedog has to go through being a puppy first, then a rambunctious adolescent, followed by a potentially very active dog, and finally, with a significant effort from the doodle owner throughout this entire growing up period of the puppy, the doodle can become the perfect dog.

Raising a doodle to his full, wonderful potential may require lifestyle changes that only you can decide if you are ready and able to make. In particular, for puppies, can you go without sleep for several days or even weeks as the pup adjusts to his new home? Are you physically active and willing to walk or jog an hour or more a day with an exuberant adolescent doodle?

For people with families: Adding a puppy to a young, growing family is a lot of work. Do you have the support of everyone in your family to help you raise the Labradoodle or Australian Labradoodle? If you have children, can you "supervise or separate" the dog and children 24 hours a day, 7 days a week?

If you are single, and used to going out on weekends or after work, are you willing to not only make arrangements for your doodle to be cared for while you are at work, but to also give up your evenings and weekends to spend time with your dog? Do you work from home, so you can be at home with the pup, adolescent, or adult dog most of the time? If not, are you financially able to afford a quality doggie day care for your doodle, or a dependable puppy/dog walker?

These are all questions you need to ask yourself, and answer them honestly. If there's a will to raise a Labradoodle or an Australian Labradoodle, there is usually a way to make it happen. But it will require commitment from you and all those in the household.

Provide the doodle with what he needs—provide him the companionship, healthcare, exercise, and mental stimulation to keep him happy—and he will return your efforts with all that he has to give: A lifetime of loyalty and unparalleled love.

Which Labradoodle Is for Me?

Now that you're considering purchasing a doodle, how do you fine tune your search to ensure that you are not only bringing home a healthy, happy puppy but also a puppy that will most closely fit your expectations for conformation, size, activity level, intelligence, trainability, and ability to adapt to your household?

One of the first decisions you need to make is whether you want the Labradoodle or the Australian Labradoodle. It's an important decision to make, as this will determine where you begin looking for your Labradoodle or AL puppy.

The F1, American Labradoodle, "designer mix," and Labradoodle all refer, of course, to the first cross between a Labrador and a Poodle. A simple Internet search will yield names and breeders around the country, as will looking in your local paper. (Caution: These listings do not ensure a quality breeder; please see "Types of Breeders," below.) Consider, too, asking your veterinarian if he or she has any recommendations for breeders. Veterinary professionals will know which breeders take excellent care of their dogs and the litters they produce. Also, check with any friends, relatives, and/or neighbors who not only rave about their Labradoodle but also rave about their breeders. You want to find the breeder who serves as a mentor, problem-solver, and friend for the lifetime of your Labradoodle.

If you are looking for a quality Australian Labradoodle, your first stop should be contacting the AL breed clubs—either the ALAA or the ALCA—and begin searching breeders near you. Both clubs have excellent websites with a breeder registry that contains information on each breeder, as well as contact information and links to their websites.

TYPES OF BREEDERS

With slick websites and beautiful photos, it may be difficult to separate the chaff from the wheat when it comes to breeders. But, with a little digging and a few phone conversations, most people will be able to uncover (or at least suspect) if a breeder is not what he or she represents.

Backyard Breeders

Backyard breeders are those who are inexperienced with breeding dogs. This individual could be a perfectly nice neighbor who happened to breed his or her family Lab to a neighbor's Poodle. Backyard breeders may have no ill intent by breeding; however, they do not health test their dogs and may not raise the puppies in a positive, healthy environment.

Puppy Mill Breeders

This is the breeder you want to avoid. It can be difficult, however, because these breeders usually are very Internet savvy, know exactly what people want to read and see, and are not above false advertisement. Some red flags to look for when you suspect a puppy mill breeder:

- The breeder sells multiple breeds and/or designer crosses.
- The breeder is selling Australian Labradoodles and is not a member of the ALAA or ALCA.
- The breeder does not health test.
- All puppies are shipped to their new owners, and local pickup is not allowed.
- If you visit the breeder and you see any of the following: Multiple breeds and crosses; poorly maintained coats and nails; dogs crated or kenneled in filthy environments; and/or outdoor only dogs.

Quality, Responsible Breeders

This breeder cares about the health, temperament, and conformation of the dogs he or she is breeding. Every breeding dog will be health tested for at least hip dysplasia and given an annual eye exam to exclude certain eye diseases.

If the breeder breeds ALs, he or she will also be a member of one of the respected Australian Labradoodle clubs—either the ALAA or the ALCA. The responsible breeder will not have his or her dogs in unfit, crowded kennels or crated in a barn. They will be in the breeder's home and/or in guardian homes.

The quality breeder is not only exceptionally knowledgeable about the breed and the dogs he or she is breeding, but this breeder is also transparent and forthcoming about

Cost

What can you expect to pay for a Labradoodle or an Australian Labradoodle?

Labradoodle: $500–$1,500
Australian Labradoodle: $2,500–$3,000

any and all health, temperament, coat, and conformation issues within his or her own lines. And, the best breeders of all will work diligently with the puppy buyer to determine the best puppy for the buyer's lifestyle and expectations, and continue as a resource for any health, behavior, training, and grooming issues for the puppy buyer. These breeders

will have glowing recommendations from puppy buyers, other breeders, and members of the veterinary community.

Don't be intimidated if your breeder asks you a lot of questions. This is a very good sign that you are working with a breeder who really cares where his or her puppies are placed.

The AL Guardianship Program

This program places breeding animals into loving pet homes, and when it is time to breed the female (or male) the adult dog is returned to the breeder for breeding. When it gets close to the female's whelping date, the females are returned to the breeder for whelping and puppy raising.

Once the puppies are raised and placed in their homes, the female dog returns to her pet home.

Depending on the Guardianship contract, a female may be required to have 2–3 litters before she can then be spayed, and become a permanent family member.

Keep in mind that the aforementioned inconveniences of having an intact female (who will come in season up to twice a year) and an intact male (potential for marking, as well as escaping to seek out females in season) will be your responsibility until the Guardianship Program requirements are fulfilled. So, this program is not for the casual pet owner but one who is willing to accept this added responsibility.

A good breeder does not want his or her puppies to fail in homes; they want them (and their owners) to be happy for a lifetime. This can only happen if you are honest with the breeder. As the saying goes, there is a solution for every problem, and with puppy raising and dog ownership that is usually the case—but you have to be honest with yourself (and the breeder) in order to recognize what your unique problems might be before you can come up with viable solutions.

If you've had no experience living with dogs and/or training dogs, your expectations

for a perfect dog may be completely unrealistic. An experienced breeder will be able to help select the best puppy for you, but you have to be very honest with the breeder about your dog experience and your lifestyle.

Knowing that you are a first-time dog owner will affect which puppy goes into your home, as well as the amount of assistance the breeder can give you prior to you bringing the puppy home.

Knowing what your lifestyle is like will not only help the breeder in selecting the best puppy to fall into your routine, but he or she can also advise what changes and sacrifices you will need to make to successfully raise your puppy.

SELECTING THE RIGHT PUP FOR YOU

So, you know what type of doodle (Labradoodle or Australian Labradoodle) you want and you've found the breeder you want to work with. Now it's time to figure out which puppy in the litter is best for you.

Do You Have a Specific Color in Mind?

Oftentimes, puppy buyers are attracted to a certain color and/or color pattern, but the puppy's temperament should be your first consideration. If a quality, reputable breeder tells you he or she has the perfect puppy that would work well with your lifestyle and your personality, put color and markings aside and consider that pup. Labradoodles and Australian Labradoodles can come in a vast range of colors and patterns, so be open to the color and markings of the puppy that is perfect for you.

Merles?

Labradoodles and Australian Labradoodles do not have a merle coat pattern. If a dog has a merle pattern, then another breed has been introduced into the mix—and none of those are approved by the AL clubs. The "Ozzie" Doodle can have a merle coat pattern; however, this is a mix of an Australian Shepherd with a Poodle. It is not to be confused with the Australian Labradoodle.

Male or Female?

If you are purchasing a Labradoodle or an Australian Labradoodle as a pet, your pup will either be altered before you bring him or her home (a common and safe practice among Australian Labradoodle breeders), or you will be required to sign a spay/neuter contract that ensures you will alter the puppy before he or she reaches sexual maturity, and then provide the breeder with proof that you have done so. Altered dogs prevent a lot of headaches—you will not have the inconveniences of a female coming in season or a male marking, howling, or running off to find what he thinks is a suitable female (i.e., any female dog in season)—unless, of course, you are purchasing a male or female under the AL Guardianship program (see "The AL Guardianship Program," page 29).

Is there a difference between the sexes? Males can be taller than females within each breed size (i.e., Miniature, Medium, Standard). Pet owners often think that the female dog is going to be the loving, doting, sweet creature they desire, but it is often the male dogs that are this way. Females can sometimes be slightly more independent and occasionally aloof. Therefore, don't prejudge a puppy's temperament until you've met the pups. And, remember to meet the breeder's dogs from whom you're purchasing your pup from. What are the breeder's male dogs like? What are the breeder's females like? That is how you'll know a little more as to whether a male or a female is the right pick for you.

If you have the ability to choose your puppy from a litter, and you're able to go to the breeder's home to meet the pups, here are some tips to help you make the best selection possible.

Meet the Parents

It sounds a bit cliché, but in all instances it is important to meet the stud and the mother of the litter to get an idea of the potential range in size, activity level, temperaments, coat types, etc., that the pups might have. Both parents should be healthy, alert, and friendly.

Observe the Puppies in Their Environment

Watch their interactions with each other. Is there one that keeps bullying his brothers and sisters? The pushy puppy could be a more dominant type and is for an experienced dog owner only—one who is willing to put in the training and leadership skills to create a good companion. Is there a puppy that seems to prefer to be alone or away from the other puppies? A retiring or shy puppy is not one for the first-time dog owner or someone who is not willing to invest a lot of time and effort to successfully bring out the best in the pup's temperament. Is there one that doesn't want to be touched or picked up? Determine whether it is just because the pup wants to return to the mass of wild puppy play or if it is because he does not like to be handled. If it is the former, you may have a very active dog with a high play drive that will require a sporting lifestyle (i.e., an owner who runs, hikes, participates in agility, etc.). If it is the latter, the puppy may not have the temperament that is suitable for a companion.

Who follows you when you walk away from the litter? There is an old breeder's saying that if a puppy picks you, you can't go wrong. If a dog has decided he wants to follow you, that means you are more interesting than anything he's ever seen. Unfortunately, most puppies are not allowed to pick their owners (some don't even meet their owners until they are delivered to them!) but know that if a puppy does pick you, you should consider taking him home.

How healthy do the puppies look? The puppies should have bright, clear eyes. They should be well fed but not possessing extended bellies (which could be an indicator of worms). Their coats should be smooth, clean, and thick with no scabs, open wounds, or sores. If it's playtime, the pups should be active, alert,

and attentive. The puppies' nails should be clipped. Their ears should pass the sniff test (no foul odor or heavy waxy discharge). And, all puppy orifices should be clean with no signs of diarrhea.

ADULT DOODLE ADOPTION

Of course, not everyone wants to acquire a young puppy or endure all the work that goes into raising an energetic, brilliant little doodle. For those who would like an adult dog, adoption is an option.

There are those breeders who will say that no well-bred Labradoodle or Australian Labradoodle will wind up in a rescue or a shelter. This simply isn't true. Dogs fail in homes everyday across the country through no fault of their own.

If you are interested in adopting an adult dog, consider looking into the many "doodle" rescues, checking with your local shelters, and visiting area SPCAs. There are lots of good dogs available that are ready to start a new life with someone. Breed rescues, and many of the shelters with better funding, provide adoptable doodles that are temperament tested, spayed/neutered, up-to-date on vaccinations, and possibly even trained in basic commands.

WHEN YOU CHOOSE, CHOOSE WISELY

When purchasing a Labradoodle, Australian Labradoodle, or anything in between, it is not the time to choose from the heart—without a little common sense from the mind. If you can find the right pup or adopt the right dog, and you're willing to put in the sweat equity necessary to transform your dog from having the potential to be a good dog to actually *being* a good dog, you will be rewarded with a lifetime of love and devotion. There's no feeling more amazing than that.

Puppy Preparations

Bringing a puppy home is exciting, but
don't forget to prepare for your new arrival.
Puppies are notorious for getting into trouble,
as they are naturally curious about their
surroundings and use their mouths to explore.

With a Labradoodle or an Australian Labradoodle puppy, you have a very curious pup with a very high IQ, and often the added high energy can put many puppy owners over the top if they aren't prepared for this.

To successfully prepare for the new puppy, you will want to make your home and yard safe, prepare for the puppy's first night in your home, and have all the necessary supplies needed for housetraining.

PUPPY-PROOFING THE HOME

If you've never raised a puppy, or it's just been a while since you had a puppy in the home, puppy-proofing your home can be a bit of a challenge. Things you think are true, such as, "oh, the puppy would never chew this" or "the puppy could never get into that space" will prove to be false 99 percent of the time. To make your home as safe as possible, start puppy-proofing from the floor up.

On the Floor

Electrical cords are a huge hazard to puppies, whether the cord is from a lamp plugged into the wall or a mess of computer wiring. If the electrical cord is active (i.e., power is flowing through the cord), the ensuing shock a puppy could receive from biting though the cord could kill him, or at least cause a serious burn, alter his heart rhythm, cause fluid collection in his lungs, and possibly even cause cataract growth.

To prevent injury to the puppy, make sure your electrical cords are up and out of reach. For those cords that cannot be secured off the floor, either run the cord underneath a rug or, if that's not possible, use a floor cord protector (found at office supply stores) to safely hide any cords or wires from your puppy.

If you have any pest or insect baits, traps, and poisons on the floor—even if they are behind a stove or a location that you think your puppy couldn't possibly reach—remove them. Your puppy will find a way to get to them and ingesting these poisons could be fatal.

Take inventory of your indoor plants, particularly those that are on the floor. Many common decorative plants are poisonous to puppies, as can be the decorative bark sometimes used in the plant's potting materials. To determine which plants are poisonous, go to the ASPCA Animal Poison Control Center (APCC), at *www.aspca.org*. The site has a listing of not only poisonous houseplants (and outdoor plants) but also what type of reaction your puppy will get from ingesting the plants. If your puppy is already home with you and you think he may have eaten something dangerous, call 888-426-4435 for a consultation over the phone 365 days a year, 24 hours a day for a small fee.

Also, be aware of the potential for poisons to drop on the floor, unnoticed to you. Classic examples of accidental poisoning include dropping a vitamin on the floor (and not finding it before your puppy does) or accidently dropping medication on the floor. If you live with anyone who has multiple medications to take on a daily basis, make sure the individual is taking his or her medications over a sink or a counter so that if a pill does happen to fall, it won't fall on the floor.

Next, move your sights to all things slightly above the floor to table height. Yes, your pup may not be big enough to reach anything on

ASPCA Poison App

Yes, there is an app for that! The ASPCA APCC has a free app for your cell phone that has the same information regarding poisonous plants as on its website.

Garage Floor Dangers

Make sure that your floor is free of any antifreeze (sweet tasting and attractive to dogs but very poisonous) that might have spilled or dripped on the floor. Battery acid spills, motor oil, paint—just about everything that you might have on the floor of your garage or on a low-lying shelf is dangerous and deadly for your puppy.

a table at the moment, but he is exceptionally intelligent and will figure out how to use chairs to get to tables soon.

So, begin with puppy-proofing your low-lying cabinets. These often contain poisonous cleaning materials. You can either use a child lock on the cabinet doors or simply use a rubber band in a figure eight pattern to lock the cabinets shut.

Remove precious trinkets from coffee tables, as your doodle puppy will surely think these are gifts for him to chew or eat. Make sure lamps have a solid base on tall tables. Fires have been started from lamps being knocked over while on and the bulbs breaking. Broken glass is also an extreme hazard, as is electrical shock.

If you leave medications on your kitchen table, stop this practice now. All medications need to be secured in high cabinets (above counter level). Your puppy will be capable of getting up on your kitchen table and childproof caps on medications are not Labradoodle or AL proof.

SAFE YARDS

When your little puppy is first home, yes, he will be so little he can't go anywhere too fast and yes, he will stay very close to you.

This only lasts for about a week. Make sure your yard has a safe, secure fence that cannot be climbed over or dug under. Fences are not inexpensive, so be sure you've budgeted for this. A chain-link fence may be the most cost effective; however, Labradoodles can climb and chain-link fencing allows for footholds or "paw" holds. A wood fence is smooth and does not allow for climbing.

Protecting Your Yard from Your Puppy

Dog urine will burn grass, so if you have areas of your backyard that you want a lush green in the summer, be sure to encourage your pup to relieve himself in a specific area that you have set up for him. You might also consider adding garden fencing around specific flower beds or vegetable gardens to keep the curious puppy out.

Then there's the question of how high is high enough for a fence. Doodles are athletic, so scaling a four-foot fence is puppy work to them. Even a 6-foot fence might not contain the largest doodles with a penchant for escaping; however, if you are in the yard at all times to supervise your doodle, and the yard is never used as a means to keep the dog out of the house, then your Labradoodle shouldn't want to climb the fence. Also, making sure your doodle is altered (spayed or neutered) will help immensely with any desire to go on a walkabout.

Already have a fence? Great! Do a walking check to make sure there are no gaps, holes, or nails protruding from your fencing.

Electric Fences

The way these fences work is that the dog receives warning shocks (through a collar) as he approaches the invisible fencing (the electric wires are buried under the ground). The shocks become increasingly strong as he approaches the barrier. While this may seem effective, there can be many problems with electric fencing: The dog must be trained on the fence; the fence must always have a power supply to it; the dog's collar must have fresh and working batteries at all times; an excited dog can blow through the barrier and bear the pain, but he won't come back inside the invisible fence; and, the invisible fence does not keep people, pets, wild animals, etc., out of your yard.

Plant and Landscaping Check

Mow the grass so it is not a haven for fleas or, depending on where you live, snakes. Make sure your trees, bushes, and flowers are not poisonous (consult the ASPCA APPC poisonous plant list at *www.aspca.org*). Additionally, if there are any areas of your yard that you do not want your puppy to relieve himself in, fence those areas off now.

Be wary, too, of any decorative mulch you are using for beds in your yard. Some types of mulch are poisonous to dogs. Some dogs will eat or swallow landscaping pebbles, so keep an eye out for this behavior, too.

Decorative water features, such as koi ponds, can be a drowning hazard. Constant supervision and/or a barrier fence will be needed for your puppy if you have a water feature.

Pools present an even bigger drowning hazard to a puppy or adult dog. If you have a pool, plan to keep it fenced off from your puppy, and teach the puppy where the steps are. Some owners will place bright orange flags to visually mark the steps for their dogs. Then, they use a dog flotation vest on the puppy to make his first swims easier and get in the pool with the puppy to teach him where to swim out.

Supplies and Equipment Checklist

✔ **Collar:** Ask your breeder what size collar to get your puppy and choose one with an easy, plastic quick-release clasp. Your puppy's first collar can be lightweight (½ inch wide) but as he grows, he will grow into a wider, 1-inch collar.

✔ **Tag:** Make a tag with your puppy's name, your city/state, and a cell phone number.

✔ **Harness:** A puppy can back out of a collar and run free with no identification. He cannot back out of a harness, and while it does allow him to pull a little easier, using a harness is the kinder way to walk a dog. (Training will keep him from pulling; see "Walk Nicely," page 86.)

✔ **Leash:** Start with a lightweight leash (½ inch is fine), as this has a small clip. Your puppy will thank you when he doesn't have a huge, brass clip banging him in the head when he goes on walks. You will want a 4-foot leash for training and a 6-foot leash for walking. Avoid purchasing a retractable leash, as these can be dangerous when wrapped around a puppy's (or your) legs, and it is virtually impossible to reel a dog in when they have hit the end of a 30-foot line.

✔ **Food:** Start your puppy off with the same food he is eating at the breeder's home. Have at least a week's supply or more in your home when he arrives. If you want to switch food later, you can over a period of time (see "Puppy Feeding Guidelines," page 50). Ask the breeder how much your puppy is eating at each meal, and use this as a starting guide.

✔ **Bowls:** Stainless steel bowls are lightweight, dishwasher safe, don't break like ceramic bowls can, don't leach potentially bad chemicals as plastic could, and are available with a rubber bottom so they don't skid across the floor.

✔ **Crate:** Your crate choices are either a wire crate, which is collapsible and has a removable pan on the bottom, or a plastic hard-shell crate that comes in two pieces (a top and a bottom). Many brands of wire crates provide a moving partition so that you can expand the puppy's living area as he grows. With the plastic hard-shell crate, you will need to purchase a puppy-sized crate, an adult-sized crate, and possibly a size in between. Plastic crates tend to be less expensive than wire crates.

✔ **Bedding:** Make your doodle's crate comfortable with a pee pad on the bottom, so

Crate Training Tips

To acclimate your puppy to his crate, make sure that it is comfortable and in a high traffic area in the home so he can see everyone and doesn't feel isolated. Also, every time he goes in the crate, make sure he has a reward, such as a chew or a treat. Keep the crate door open even when he doesn't need to be in the crate so that it is always a welcome retreat for him.

And, perhaps most importantly, never associate the crate with a "bad" thing, such as a "time out." Even if you must place him in the crate while you clean up a mess, calm yourself first, and when you place him in the crate, do so with gentleness, love, and a treat.

if there is an accident, it doesn't get all over the crate. Then, layer a soft towel or a sturdy packing blanket to the crate, but be sure to watch your puppy—some puppies will suck and chew on towels and blankets, creating choking hazards. Avoid plush crate pads until you know whether your puppy is a shredder or not, as the fill-in crate pads and dog beds can also be a choking hazard.

✔ **Pet Gates:** Pet gates come in all shapes, materials, and sizes. They can be heavy-duty, permanent doorway gates or moveable pressure gates. Whichever gate you choose, they are an excellent way to keep your pup safely in one area.

✔ **X-Pen:** A large exercise pen (x-pen) that is tall enough that the puppy cannot jump out for several months is a great way to keep him comfortable when you can't keep eyes directly on him and you don't want to add to his crate time.

✔ **Toys and Chews:** Labradoodle and AL puppies can be big chewers. Depending on the size of your puppy and what size he will be when fully grown, choose toys and chews that are size appropriate and won't be a swallowing hazard. Avoid plush, stuffed toys that can easily be gutted and go with puppy-sized Kongs, Greenies, and other safe chews.

✔ **Housetraining Supplies**: Have a supply of puppy pee pads (or washable whelping pads) and cleaning materials (including a product that breaks down enzymes to rid carpets, upholstery, floors, etc., of stains and odor).

FIRST NIGHT SURVIVAL TIPS

The adage to "just let your puppy cry" doesn't hold water among animal behaviorists today. The recommendation now is if your puppy is crying, determine the cause of your puppy's crying and solve the problem. It is less stressful to the puppy, and you will get a better night's sleep with a calm, restful puppy.

So, why do puppies cry for their first night in a new home? Well, for one, they are baby dogs who have spent their entire being living with the their littermates and their mother. They are used to sleeping in a huge puppy pile, and now they are in a strange place, away from their mother and away from their siblings. You would cry, too.

If your puppy is crying because he is lonely, sleep with him. Don't ostracize him to the laundry room. Bring his crate into your bedroom, right next to your bed where he can see you, and let him sleep there. Many owners will bring out the guest air mattress and settle in on the floor, right next to the puppy.

Resist the temptation to bring the puppy in bed with you. Not because the puppy wouldn't enjoy it (he would), but because he may relieve himself in your bed. Or, he may fall off your bed and seriously injure himself. Also, if you are a heavy sleeper, you could roll over in your sleep and crush him. Let him sleep in his crate next to you, for now.

Your puppy may also cry because he is cold. He is sleeping by himself for the first time in his life, and he isn't getting any heat from a pile of puppies. To help him keep warm, make sure his crate has nice, soft towels or a moving blanket and is free of drafts. Consider putting a hot water bottle with warm (not scalding) water under a few layers of towels.

Your puppy could be hungry. Make sure to keep him on a regular feeding schedule. You can also put a chewy bone in his crate or a Kong stuffed with peanut butter for him to chew on, much like a pacifier to help him go to sleep.

Some scents can be calming to an anxious puppy, too, such as Dog Appeasing Pheromone (DAP). This product replicates the hormone that is given off by a nursing female dog, and your puppy will find it calming. It can be sprayed (a little goes a long way) in the puppy's crate or on his bedding.

Your puppy may also be crying because he could have to relieve himself. The longer it takes him to fall asleep and the more active or stressed he is, the faster his body will metabolize any water he drank before he was crated and he will have to relieve himself sooner.

Above all, stay calm for your puppy. Pay attention to his needs and he should be fine. Your Labradoodle is only a puppy once. Take time to enjoy the little guy.

Teaching a dog where to relieve himself (and where not to relieve himself) can seem difficult and at times frustrating; however, it really is pretty simple. Dogs live by a few basic rules. If you understand your dog's natural instincts and understand the principles of positive reinforcement and repetition, housetraining is not difficult. It does require time, patience, and realistic expectations.

Sense of Space

Your puppy is born with a natural instinct not to soil his "den." Your puppy wants to keep his area clean. The puppy's idea of "his area," however, may be much smaller than what your idea might be. For example, a puppy will not soil his bed unless he has nowhere else to go. If he is in a small crate that only has room for his bed, he will try to "hold" as long as he can. If he is in a large crate, he may consider his "space" one corner of the crate and be perfectly okay with relieving himself in the other corner and won't attempt to "hold" anything at all.

So, your job is to create a space that is big enough for him to be comfortable relaxing and sleeping yet small enough that he wants to avoid eliminating until you let him out.

Setting Realistic Expectations

The puppy's ability to "hold" is directly related to his age. A relatively calm puppy that has fully relieved himself prior to resting in the crate should be comfortable for as many hours (up to 8) that the puppy is old in months. For example, a 2-month-old puppy should be able to rest for 2 hours. A 4-month-old puppy should be able to rest for 4 hours.

Total time in a crate, however, should never exceed 8 hours in a 24-hour period, even as an adult.

Know the Signs

A puppy presents very distinctive body language that indicates he needs to relieve himself. Know these signs so you can quickly get him outside.
- Sudden stop in play
- Sniffing
- Spinning in a circle
- Running away/behind something

Know the Top Five Relief Times

These times are an absolute given that your puppy will need to relieve himself. Be sure to always offer him the opportunity to go outside:
- After/during hard play: This includes when you are playing fetch in the kitchen or having a wild game of tug.
- Within 20 minutes of eating: Food in, food byproducts out. For some puppies, it's not even a 20-minute period—as soon as they have finished eating, it is time to go out.
- Within an hour of drinking: If you've come back from a walk and your puppy drank quite a bit of water, you can expect that he will need to relieve himself within the hour.
- As soon as you let him out of his crate: He has been "holding" in his crate, so the very minute you let him out, take him immediately (or even carry him) outside, as he will need to go right away.
- Upon waking: Whether he spent the night in the crate and he is being let out, or if he

is older and spent the night cuddled with you in your bed, when he wakes up he will need to relieve himself. With older puppies and adolescents, this means you need to let them out as soon as they get up. You can't wait to shower, put on a pair of shorts, or even lace up your shoes. The first order of the day is to get the Labradoodle or AL out to the yard.

Use Positive Reinforcement Only

Calmly praise the puppy every time he relieves himself in the proper place outside.

Teach him a "go potty" command, saying it right as he is circling or starting to squat to relieve himself outside. Praise him when he relieves himself. He will learn the command,

which is helpful when you're in a rush to get to work, or it's storming outside and you really need him to GO and GO NOW.

Never punish him after-the-fact for relieving himself in the home. It does not work. He won't understand he's done anything wrong and really, the accident is your fault. You either made him hold too long, weren't watching for signs he needed to relieve himself, weren't supervising him closely enough, or gave him too much space too soon.

The only time it could be even remotely permissible to raise your voice with your pup is if he is in mid-stream and you catch him. Then and only then can you say, "Ah ah," then pick him up gently, run him outside, and then praise him.

Labradoodle Basic Care

Many things in life that affect the longevity of your doodle cannot be controlled. The few things that you *can* control are the quality of your pup's food, good grooming practices, and preventive veterinary care.

GOOD NUTRITION AND BASIC FOOD CHOICES

Walking down the aisle of a pet care superstore and trying to pick the right food can be overwhelming. Dog foods are made for every stage of life, for different sizes of dogs, and for specific breeds of dogs, as well as to treat health problems. If you are dazed by the choices, you are not alone.

Although your first instinct may be to reach for a budget food, don't. Inexpensive dog foods are not a healthy choice or a wise financial decision. Foods with little nutritional value are chock full of fillers that cannot be digested properly by your dog. It will take bigger portions (and more money) to reach your pup's minimum nutritional needs. All this extra food will create more "output" by your doodle, too, which means more pick up duties for you. And, regarding that beautiful Labradoodle coat . . . poor nutrition from cheap dog food will not make his coat shine.

So, to find the perfect food for your pup or adult, start by looking for one that has met the Association of American Feed Control Official's (AAFCO) nutritional requirements for either a puppy (labeled as "growth") or an adult ("maintenance"), or all ages ("all life stages").

The AAFCO created its most recent pet food standards in 2016, which includes not only minimum nutritional requirements but maximum requirements as well. To determine if the food you want to use meets these standards, and for the quality of the food's ingredients, look on the product's label for key information.

"Complete and Balanced" These words indicate that the pet food not only contains all the nutrients needed for a healthy diet but that they are also present in the correct ratios.

"[Name of food] is formulated to meet the nutritional levels established by the AAFCO Dog Food Nutrient Profiles for [stage of life]." This statement relates that the food has been tested in a laboratory and contains the required nutrients in the correct amount for a dog in a particular life stage. What this doesn't test is the palatability of the food (do dogs like to eat it?) or if the dogs can metabolize the nutrients.

"Animal feeding tests using AAFCO procedures substantiate that [name of food] provides complete and balanced nutrition for the [life stage]." This sentence indicates that the food was tested with feeding trials rather than tested in a laboratory. The food is palatable and dogs are receiving the nutrients in a digestible form. It is more expensive to perform feeding trials, but this is the food you want to consider for your doodle.

Ingredients

The AAFCO also established guidelines as to how food manufacturers can label the ingredients used to make their foods.

- Meat/poultry is the muscle tissue that is skeletal, or found in the tongue, diaphragm, heart, and esophagus.
- Meat by-product may contain: non-rendered, cleaned parts *other than meat* (*muscle tissue*), and includes internal organs and bones.

Therapeutic Diets

Foods prescribed by your veterinarian for a specific health problem are not required to provide a statement of nutritional adequacy. If your veterinarian prescribes a therapeutic food for your dog, there is a strong reason for it, and your veterinarian will be able to tell you more about the contents of the food.

- Poultry by-product is similar to meat by-product, as it contains the non-rendered, cleaned parts of the chicken or turkey that is not muscle tissue and includes the heart, gizzard and liver (giblets), internal organs, and heads and feet.

  Other terms:
- "Rendered" refers to the process of cooking with high heat and pressure to destroy harmful bacteria and remove most of the meat's water content and fat, creating a product that is shipped to pet food manufacturers that contains primarily protein and minerals.
- The term "meal" is used to identify products that, in addition to being cooked, are ground to form uniform-sized particles.

What's Best?

The highest quality foods will list a meat or poultry (beef, lamb, salmon, chicken, turkey, etc.) as the first ingredient on the bag. Additionally, some foods have gone to using "human grade" ingredients, which hold the food sourcing to a higher standard than those used in pet foods—so you may see this on a food label.

Cost is often an indicator of quality with dog foods, as the higher-grade ingredients, digestible vitamins and minerals, and feeding trials all cost more. For example, over a lifetime of eating top-grade, quality dog food that costs $60 a month to feed (30-pound bag of kibble), if your doodle lives to be 15, you will have spent $10,800 in food alone. If you feed wet foods (canned), your expenses will be even higher.

Types of Packaged Foods

Dry: Packaged as small bits of kibble, this food is the most economical to buy and store, and it has a long shelf life. Dry kibble can also help with keeping a dog's teeth clean, if the dog chews his food. Dogs that swallow their food whole will not get any dental benefit from dry foods.

Semi-moist: This commercial food is designed to be chewy or have chewy bits in it. Typically, it is higher in unnecessary salts and sugars.

Wet: Canned foods contain fresher nutrients than dry foods; however, they have a higher percentage of water, making it proportionately costlier. Opened cans need to be refrigerated. It can be expensive to feed a dog strictly with wet foods, particularly for dogs more than 40 pounds. It is a great kibble topper, however.

Powdered: These foods are dehydrated, typically human-grade foods that are then reduced to a powder form and boxed. A 10-pound box of powdered food, when mixed with warm water, will make 40 pounds of

Food Allergies

According to a recent study, beef was the largest source for food allergies (95 percent), followed by dairy. Research indicates that the most common food allergies among dogs are as follows: beef, dairy, wheat, egg, chicken, lamb, soy, pork, rabbit, and fish, and that commonly dogs with food allergies were allergic to more than one source of protein. Food allergies build up with exposure, so often a dog will not immediately start itching or scratching, develop red skin, and/or suffer ear infections overnight.

food. The powdered foods come as either a full meal, or as a dog food "base." The base food is to be mixed with a protein of the owner's choice. These foods store well, as you only prepare with warm water what you need for each meal. The texture is different from what most dogs will have seen and may (or may not) take adjusting to by the dog.

Fresh, refrigerated rolls: These foods have a short shelf life and require refrigeration at all times. Packaged as rolls, fresh, refrigerated dog food rolls are highly palatable but more expensive than dry foods. Refrigerated food rolls can be used as food toppers for kibble.

Freeze-dried: Foods that have been freeze-dried and packaged usually are wet foods that contain raw meat. Water can be added to the food, if a dog tends not to hydrate well, or it can be fed as is. Because

this food contains raw foods, owners are advised to practice safe food handling. (See "Raw Foods," page 48.)

Frozen: Frozen dog foods are typically commercially prepared raw diets (see "Raw Foods," page 48) and require freezer space, as well as safe food handling practices. Some research indicates, too, that the "hard" freeze required for these foods effectively kills off harmful bacteria.

Specialty Foods and Diets

Pet owners are always seeking a better or healthier way to feed their dogs. From this desire, multiple specialty and/or alternative diets have been developed by pet food companies.

Grain-free Foods: Many dogs do very well on grain-free diets; however, if you are trying to control a dog's allergies with a grain-free product, you may be surprised to find that grains are not the most common form of allergies (see "Food Allergies," left), but rather animal proteins are.

Grain-free diets came into fashion as pet owners were seeking a food that was more "natural," with proponents arguing that ancestors of today's dogs did not eat grain. This may be true; however, today's dogs have evolved to digest grains, as well as what many grain-free foods use in their formula as a substitute for grains—the equally as "unnatural" substitute, potatoes.

Is a grain-free diet what your dog should be eating? If your doodle does well on a grain-free diet, then yes, it's a good food for him. Many of the grain-free diets are produced as premium, high-quality dog foods with excellent sources of highly-digestible nutrition. So, whether you're trying to feed a more "natural" diet or just a really high-quality diet, a grain-free diet could be the ticket.

Gluten-free Foods: A gluten-free dog food means the food is free of wheat, a source of protein, and a source of allergens for some dogs. Keep in mind that "gluten free" is not the same as grain-free; a food that does not contain wheat but does contain corn, for example, is a gluten-free food. There are, however, gluten-free and grain-free foods available for dogs. A gluten-free food may benefit your dog if he has food-based allergies, as wheat is one of the top three foods that cause allergies in dogs.

Limited-ingredient Foods: These dog foods can be dry or wet and usually limit the ingredients to a single source animal protein and the most essential, natural ingredients. Limited-ingredient foods are often marketed to dogs with sensitive systems, and typically are grain and gluten free, and have no artificial colorings, flavorings, or preservatives.

Natural Foods: Often very similar in makeup to the limited-ingredient foods, "natural" foods promote healthy ingredients and have no artificial colorings, flavorings, or preservatives.

Raw Foods: These pet foods contain raw, uncooked proteins. Raw foods can be purchased in a freeze-dried form or in a frozen package. If creating a raw diet at home, dog owners often refer to the BARF diet (Bones and Raw Foods or Biologically Appropriate Raw Foods).

Raw Food Caution

Some raw foods can be contaminated with dangerous bacteria, such as *Salmonella*, and/or disease-causing pathogens, such as *Listeria monocytogenes*. In fact, in a recent study that spanned two years of testing, the FDA Center for Veterinary Medicine (CVM) found that, compared to other types of pet food tested, raw pet food was much more likely to be contaminated with disease-causing bacteria than any other pet foods. Additionally, several recent studies have linked hyperthyroidism (an extremely rare condition of the thyroid producing too much hormone) in dogs that were fed raw diets. Researchers believe there is a link between dogs eating the meaty bones of necks of animals as part of their diet and hyperthyroidism. The raw animal necks or treats contain neck and thyroid tissue that can cause hyperthyroidism in dogs.

The FDA CVM warns owners to be aware of the risks, and to follow safe food handling practices, as provided below:

- Thoroughly wash your hands with soap and water (for at least 20 seconds) after handling raw pet food and after touching surfaces or objects that have come in contact with the raw food.
- Thoroughly clean and disinfect all surfaces and objects that come in contact with raw pet food. First wash with hot soapy water, and then follow with a disinfectant. You can also run items through the dishwasher after each use to clean and disinfect them.
- Freeze raw meat and poultry products until you are ready to use them, and thaw them in your refrigerator or microwave, not on your countertop or in your sink.
- Carefully handle raw and frozen meat and poultry products. Don't rinse raw meat, poultry, fish, and seafood. Bacteria in the raw juices can splash and spread to other food and surfaces.
- Keep raw food separate from other food.
- Immediately cover and refrigerate what your pet doesn't eat, or throw out the leftovers safely.
- If you're using raw ingredients to make your own *cooked* pet food, be sure to cook all food to a proper internal temperature as measured by a food thermometer. Thorough cooking kills *Salmonella, L. monocytogenes*, and other harmful foodborne bacteria.
- Don't kiss your pet around his mouth, and don't let your pet lick your face. This is especially important after your pet has just finished eating raw food.
- Thoroughly wash your hands after touching or being licked by your pet. If your pet gives you a "kiss," be sure to also wash your face.

Home-prepared diet: Homemade food is prepared using fresh ingredients that can be purchased at a grocery and cooked proteins (not raw), as well as supplements to correctly balance the diet. If you have the time and energy and refrigerator/freezer storage to prepare and safely keep batches of food for your dog, this could be a very healthy way to feed your doodle.

With that said, veterinarians say the number one reason homemade diets fail is that dog owners start off well, but then they begin cutting corners and making substitutions. If you are interested in home cooking a diet for your dog, consult your veterinarian for a

Dangerous People Food

The following foods can cause reactions ranging from mild to potentially deadly and should never be offered to your Labradoodle.

- Chocolate
- Garlic
- Almonds, Macadamia nuts
- Apple seeds, cranberries, prunes, rhubarb, grapes, raisins
- High fatty foods (if dog is prone to pancreatitis)
- Caffeine
- Artificial sweeteners, including sorbitol, stevia, sucralose, xylitol

complete and balanced recipe and a source for the supplements. You may also be interested in looking into the company Balance It (*www.balanceit.com*). In addition to selling recipes and supplements that are easy to include in a home prepared diet, this veterinarian-owned business also provides an online service for building your own meals with your dog's favorite protein source and vegetables, allowing you to mix up what you feed him while ensuring the diet is always perfectly balanced.

PUPPY FEEDING GUIDELINES

How much should you feed your puppy? The best source for determining your puppy's current serving size is by asking your breeder

Adopted Doodle Feeding Recommendations

If you have adopted an adult dog, you can follow the same feeding guidelines as noted above for feeding the puppy: Begin by feeding the dog the recommended serving for his size and age on the pet food container. Feed in a non-competitive environment to allow the dog to eat what he wants and to avoid other dogs from stealing his food. See how much he eats in 30 minutes and pick up his food. Note: if your adopted Labradoodle is thin or obese, his feeding requirements will differ. It is best to begin with the package directions, but consult your veterinarian for more tailored feeding advice.

how much your puppy is eating at every meal. If the breeder only knows an approximate amount (puppies eat out of a communal bowl, so it can be hard to know exactly), you can follow a few steps to make sure your puppy is receiving enough food but not being encouraged to overeat.

Start by feeding the suggested amount for your puppy's size and age that is recommended by the makers of the puppy food you are feeding. (This information is printed on the bag.) Pick up your puppy's food after 30 minutes and measure what he left in the bowl. Continue feeding and measuring to get an idea of how much your puppy is eating and adjust his serving size appropriately. Be advised that your puppy will need an increasing amount of food as he grows into an adolescent.

ADULT FEEDING TIPS

Once your doodle has reached maturity (between nine months and one year) he can be switched over to a quality adult food. As your doodle goes through his adult years, your biggest concern will be watching that he doesn't become overweight. Canine obesity is not uncommon; in fact, the Association for Pet Obesity Prevention (APOP) estimates that nearly 53 percent of adult dogs are over-weight and nearly 20 percent are obese.

Excess weight can cause osteoarthritis, insulin resistance and type 2 diabetes, high blood pressure, heart and respiratory disease, cranial cruciate ligament injury, kidney disease, many forms of cancer, and a decreased life expectancy (up to 2.5 years).

If you find that your doodle is gaining weight, you have a few choices to reverse the situation.

- You can continue feeding the same food, but feed your dog a smaller portion, adding green beans, pumpkin, and other tummy fillers that have nutritional value without the calories.
- You can change your dog's food to a lower caloric food, such as a weight loss food.
- Instead of feeding one meal a day, you can try feeding smaller meals more frequently.
- If you're using treats for training, try substituting a portion of the dog's food as his training treats.
- Exercise your dog—not just a leisurely stroll. Walk or jog with purpose on the way out, then if you want to walk leisurely on the way back, you can. Time your dog's exercise to the time he is most likely to beg. This can be a great way to distract him, and he will love the interaction.
- Substitute play for when your dog begs for food. As you might suspect, dogs can substitute food for affection, so try playing with your dog first before you feed him. If your dog's bowl is empty, and you've already played with him and exercised him and it's not quite meal time, try adding just a few kibbles to his bowl.
- Offer your dog crunchy treats that have nutrition but are low calorie, such as raw baby carrots, broccoli, celery, and asparagus.
- And, don't forget to offer your dog a drink of fresh, cool water. Sometimes that is what your dog really wants.

EXERCISE: A TIRED DOODLE IS A GOOD DOODLE

Exercise is not only a way for your puppy or adult dog to burn off excess energy, it also provides your Labradoodle or Australian Labradoodle with mental stimulation. In fact, exercise stimulates all of your dog's senses!

Little puppies will be perfectly happy with a 20-minute walk and play time in the kitchen and backyard. Older puppies will require an increasing amount of exercise. By the age of 6 months, you may find that the only way to keep your growing puppy's energy needs met is to walk an hour three times a day, along with a solid, all out run in the yard. That's in the case of a very high-energy dog. A medium-energy dog will still benefit from an hour of walking (maybe in two 30-minute sessions)

as well as all out running in a fenced yard. A low-energy Labradoodle—oh wait, there's no such thing. Sorry!

Exercise should not be confused with the multiple training sessions you will have with your puppy on a *daily* basis (more on this in Chapter 8: "Training Basics," pages 76–89).

ACTIVITIES FOR THE DOODLE

With the athleticism of the Labradoodle and the Australian Labradoodle, and the dog's intelligence and ease of training, it would be a shame not to get involved in one of the many activities that doodles excel in.

Whether you want to perform a civil service by volunteering your time with your dog as a therapy dog, or if you have a competitive streak and want to compete in a dog sport with your doodle, or maybe something in between, there is an activity for you and your doodle.

The Good Deeds Doodle

Want to start your Labradoodle or AL off on the right paw? A great place to start is with the American Kennel Club (AKC) puppy program.

S.T.A.R. Puppy: Attend a basic puppy training class that is certified as a S.T.A.R. (Socialization, Training, Activity, Responsibility) puppy program and learn basic training and puppy-raising troubleshooting. Pass the test at the end of the class, and your pup will receive a certification.

Canine Good Citizen (CGC): This test requires you and your dog to pass ten different tasks, such as "sitting politely for petting," and "walking through a crowd." Upon passing the test, your Labradoodle will receive a certificate of his title.

Community Canine (CGCA): Taking the CGC one step further with the Canine Good Citizen Advanced (CGCA), this test not only requires the dog to perform certain tasks and commands, but it also tests his manners in public environments, such as pet stores, dog shows, or community settings.

Therapy Dog: Dog and handler teams can serve as therapy dog teams, usually involved in one of two ways:

- Therapeutic Visitation Dog: The handler and dog volunteer as a team to visit patients in a variety of facilities: hospitals and hospices, nursing homes, veterans' centers, Alzheimer's facilities, and schools (Read To Me program). In other settings, doodles can also serve as "comfort" dogs that assist people in courtrooms (e.g., when a child is testifying as a witness in a criminal court) and those who suffer from traumatic events, such as mass shootings, terrorist attacks, and natural disasters.
- Animal Assisted Therapy Dog: The dog and handler therapy team are part of a patient's treatment plan, whether that is to encourage a patient to regain mobility, strength, range of motion, balance, and/or confidence. The team works directly with a health facility's physical and occupational therapists.

Organizations that test and certify dogs for therapy work include: Pet Partners (*www. petpartners.org*), Therapy Dogs United (*www.therapydogsunited.org*), and Therapy Dogs International (*www.tdi-dog.org*). Each organization has its own requirements, but all require a calm, well trained, friendly, and highly tolerant dog, along with an equally as friendly handler. Contact the organizations for more information, or ask local therapy dog handler teams who they were certified with and which organization they work under.

The Performance Doodle

Looking for a mentally challenging sport for your Labradoodle or Australian Labradoodle, as well as the opportunity to win awards and prizes? Check out the following canine performance events to see if any might be up your doodle's alley.

Agility: In this sport, the handler directs the doodle through a series of course obstacles, such as jumps, ramps, weave poles, tunnels, and teeter totters. Within each competition, there are several different class types, with each class testing a different skill set, such as accuracy, fastest time, strategy, and distance handling. Organizations that hold agility events include the AKC, Canine Performance Events, Inc. (CPE), North American Dog Ability Council (NADAC), United Kennel Club (UKC), and the United States Dog Agility Association (USDAA).

Disc Dog: This sport was made famous in 1974 when a college student, Alex Stein, smuggled his whippet, Ashley, into a nationally televised baseball game, jumped a fence, and threw a Frisbee to his dog for eight minutes before he was escorted off the field. Now, disc dogs no longer have to crash professional baseball games to gain notoriety; there are several different organizations offering competitions: *www.skyhoundz.com*, *www.ufoworldcup.org*, and *www.ashleywhippet.com*.

DockDogs: Billed as the "World's Premier Canine Aquatics Competition," DockDogs

holds events around the country and encourages all dog owners to participate and have fun. Currently, the individual events that DockDogs holds include Big Air, Speed Retrieve, and Extreme Vertical, as well as a combined event called Iron Dog. The principle behind the fun is that dogs leap off of a platform into a huge pool of water to retrieve a fetch toy. The sport is open to any dog of any age and any breeding. For more information, contact DockDogs at *www.dockdogs.com*. The UKC also holds dock jumping events (*www.ukcdogs.com*).

Flyball: Flyball is a relay race in which two teams, of four dogs each, race over a 51-foot course, jumping hurdles along the way. Each dog must run the length of the course, trigger a box that releases a ball in the air, catch the ball, and race back over to the start line—where the next dog takes off to do exactly the same thing. The first team

of dogs to have all four dogs finish the course wins that heat. For more information on this sport, contact the North American Flyball Association (NAFA) at *www.flyball.org*.

The Obedient Doodle

Interested in training your doodle in traditional obedience? Or, maybe you might be interested in Rally, which is considered a very fun stepping stone to formal obedience trials. Whatever your level of interest, your Labradoodle can excel!

Rally: A rally course has 10 to 20 stations that require the dog and handler to perform a different skill or exercise at each station. Skills could include, "sit-stay," "change pace," or "make a U-turn." The fun part of this competition is that you can talk to your dog the entire time, offer him encouragement, and praise him. Scoring is not as rigorous, and the intent is for dog and handler to have fun. Organizations that offer Rally include the World Cynosport Rally (*www.rallydogs.com*), the AKC, and the UKC.

Obedience: Obedience is one of the oldest dog sports in the U.S., dating back to the 1930s. Today, dogs and handlers can participate in obedience trials either non-competitively (working toward passing the specific level of test three times in order to pass that level), or competing to be awarded the highest score in a trial or a class award. The level at which you participate depends on the pressure you put on yourself. Obedience trials are held by the AKC and the UKC.

GROOMING YOUR LABRADOODLE

Everyday grooming tools for your doodle will include a quality pin brush, a comb, a dematting blade, and a nail clipper. Additional supplies include a grooming table with an arm and drop-down loop to hold your doodle in place, scissors, quality dog shampoos and conditioners, and a commercial grade blow dryer that has a warm (not hot) setting.

Brushing

The different coat types of the Labradoodle and AL require different groom-ing regimes. The hair coat, which sheds, does not mat but does require brushing to stimu-late healthy skin and to minimize shed hair. Fleece and wool coats mat and require much more than a cursory brushing.

With fleece and wool coats, you will need to use a pin brush. Do not purchase the pin brushes that have a round ball attached to the end of the pin; although less expensive, they are difficult to work with and can get caught up in the dog's coat, causing more problems.

When brushing, pay special attention to the areas of the coat prone to matting, such as behind the ears, around the neck, and in the dog's armpits, neck, and tail. If he wears a harness, check anywhere the harness rubs, such as on his chest and across his shoulders.

Brush your doodle's coat thoroughly. Make a part in his coat and brush through the entire length of the coat from the skin to the tip of the hairs. Once this line of hair is clear of mats and tangles, make a new part a couple of inches from where your last part was. Clear this area of mats and tangles. Continue until you've brushed through his entire coat.

Dematting

First, try to pick the mat out with a comb. Some mats are small and your comb should

pick up the little tangle of coat hairs and remove it from the surrounding hairs. Doing this will give your dog's skin a little tug, so hold the coat hairs at the base of the mat and then pull the mat out.

Bigger mats will require the use of a dematting tool. This tool has several, very sharp, hooked, stainless steel blades on one end. The blades catch into the mat and slice the hairs apart. Once the big mat has been made into smaller mats, you can use a comb to remove the individual pieces. A hollow mat can be removed by grasping either side of the mat and pulling the hairs apart. Then, rotate your hands 45 degrees and grasp the mat again and pull it apart. Keep rotating back and forth until the mat gives and pulls completely apart.

Serious mats? That's when it's time to go to a professional and have the mat clipped out.

Nails

If your doodle has clear nails, it is easy to see where the quick (blood supply) is, as it is

pink. You will want to clip the nail so that it is close to the pink, but not so close that it actually causes him discomfort or, worse yet, that you cut into the quick and make him bleed.

If you have a dog with black nails, it is a bit harder; however, there are some ways to determine where the quick in the nail is. Look at the underside of the nail and the spot where the nail goes from being a solid, smooth nail to where it separates into a triangular-shaped wedge. This is where the quick begins. Position your nail clippers a little farther into the smooth part of the nail, and make a 45-degree clip (from the bottom of the nail angled toward the end of the nail, so that the bottom of the nail is slightly shorter than the top of the nail).

If clipping your dog's nails makes you nervous, it will make your doodle nervous, too. Your veterinary clinic or your groomer will be able to do this for you.

Ears

If your doodle is a frequent swimmer, you will want to invest in an ear drying solution. This solution is used after baths and helps prevent bacterial and fungal infections from occurring. Put a few drops in each ear and massage for several seconds. Then, wipe out the solution and any ear wax with a cotton ball, and allow him to shake his head.

Make sure to smell his ears on a regular basis, too. A healthy ear shouldn't smell. An infected ear will have a distinctive odor. If you detect a change in the ears' odor, see a lot of wax in the dogs ears, or see any any inflammation (the inside of the ear and flap are red), take your doodle to the veterinarian

Bathing Frequency

You can wash your doodle as often as weekly when using a shampoo that doesn't strip the coat of its oils. If your doodle swims in lakes or the ocean, you should bathe your doodle after every swim. A doodle that doesn't swim or dirty his coat will only need bathing once a month or so.

as soon as possible. These are signs of an ear infection.

Bathing

With a young puppy, it's good to at least wet and blow dry your puppy once a week so that he gets used to bathing.

When washing your doodle, use water that is a comfortable temperature. It should not be ice cold or be scalding hot. Completely wet your doodle before applying shampoo. Pick a shampoo that is made for dogs and is tearless. Work the shampoo through to the skin. Wash the soap from the dog's coat, and rinse him thoroughly again.

Use towels to get him as dry as you can. Then, blow dry and brush out the rest of his coat until it's dry. Make sure to completely dry your doodle—wet hairs close to the skin will mat.

Trimming

Not all doodles will require trimming of their coats, but some doodles may have a neater appearance if their coats are trimmed. All doodles will, however, require the pads

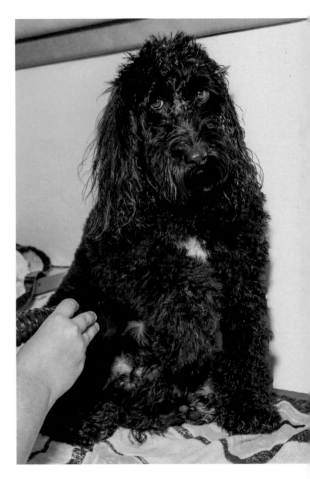

of their feet to be trimmed so that they aren't running on huge, slick hair slippers. This is most easily accomplished by using a small mustache/beard trimmer and clipping the bottom of the foot, being careful not to catch any of the pad in the clipper blades.

The other must-trim area for a doodle is under his tail. Keeping this area clear of hair will keep feces from drying and building up.

Puppy's First Exam

One of the greatest things you can do for your puppy's health and longevity is to plan for regular health exams, beginning with his well-puppy physical.

To start your puppy off right, you will need to find a veterinarian and schedule your puppy's first appointment within the first few days of bringing him home.

HOW TO FIND A VETERINARIAN

If you've owned dogs before, you likely have a veterinarian whom you use and trust. If you haven't owned a dog before or if you live in a new area, you may need to search for a veterinary clinic.

You can start by asking your breeder (if he or she is local) to recommend a veterinarian in the area. If you have friends with healthy, happy dogs, ask them who they go to and what they like about their veterinarians. You can also go online and search for veterinarians in your area. And, while you're online, check out the American Animal Hospital Association (AAHA) website (*www.aaha.org*) for a list of accredited veterinary hospitals in your area.

When you go to the veterinarian's office, carry your puppy in, as he is unvaccinated and susceptible to disease until he has completed his puppy series. Even though veterinary clinics and hospitals take great care to sanitize the floors every day, many ill dogs walk across the floor, lie down, lick, drool, may have a discharge, or relieve themselves. Why risk it?

Once you get into the exam room, your puppy will be weighed and his temperature taken.

Your veterinarian will check the overall health of the puppy. The puppy's exam will include a physical check of all joints, paws

Temperature Check

If you'd like to learn how to check your puppy's temperature, the veterinarian technician will be able to show you. It's good to have this skill, because if your puppy becomes ill, the first thing you will want to check is his temperature.

and pads, orifices, eyes, ears, and a check for teeth and how the bite is coming in. Your veterinarian will palpate your pup's abdominal area to check for any abnormalities or signs of discomfort. And, he will listen to the puppy's heart and lungs.

Bring all the records of vaccinations and dewormings that your breeder gives to you. Also, bring a fresh stool sample to the clinic. The clinic will test your puppy's stool sample for the presence of worms. It is not uncommon for a pup to have worms (see "Controlling Parasites," page 61), so you may receive a dewormer to give him when you get home. Your veterinarian will also give you a heartworm preventive that is safe for puppies and is based on your puppy's weight at that appointment. (A larger dose will be given at one of his next appointments.) Whether your puppy receives any vaccinations at this appointment is dependent on what age he is and what vaccinations he has already received from the breeder.

Most veterinary clinics hand out puppy packets with quite a bit of information and samples. Often, the packet will include a beginner tooth brushing kit, so you can start acclimating your puppy to having his teeth cleaned regularly. If you don't receive a kit, you can pick one up at your local pet product store. The kit will include a finger brush and toothpaste made specifically for dogs. Do not use human toothpaste, as it is dangerous for dogs. (Dogs can't spit, so they cannot have the same chemicals in their toothpaste.)

RECOMMENDED VACCINATIONS

When with your veterinarian, he or she will discuss what vaccinations are recommended for your puppy. Typically, all puppies receive their "core" vaccinations beginning at the age of 6 or 8 weeks and continuing every 3–4 weeks until the series is complete. The puppy will then be given a "booster" vaccination at age 1, and then every 3 years.

Core vaccinations are given to prevent the following diseases:
- Canine Parvovirus (CPV)
- Distemper Virus
- Adenovirus-2

Additionally, a killed rabies vaccine is mandated by state law to be given between 12 weeks and 6 months, depending on the state you live in. A rabies booster is given one year after the puppy's first rabies vaccination, and then (again, depending on the state) a rabies booster is required every 1 to 3 years. Your veterinarian will know what your state's requirements are.

NON-CORE VACCINATIONS

Non-core vaccines are optional. Your veterinarian will discuss the risks in your area, versus the potential side effects of these

Allergic Reactions to Vaccinations

A pup is at most risk for an allergic reaction within the first 48 hours after receiving a vaccine. Reactions may include, vomiting and/or diarrhea within the first few hours of vaccine administrations, as well as puffiness around the eyes, muzzle, and ears. Dogs can also develop hives or bumps on their bodies. And, an extremely rare but deadly reaction is an anaphylactic reaction in which the tongue and airways of the dog swell, cutting off the dog's supply of oxygen. Allergic reactions to core vaccinations are rare, but some veterinarians will ask that you stay at the clinic for up to 20 minutes after your puppy is inoculated, just to watch for a severe reaction.

If your puppy has a reaction to any of his vaccines, even if it is mild, tell your veterinarian. He or she needs to be aware of this for future vaccinations.

vaccines. With every health choice, the benefits need to outweigh the potential adverse reactions.

Kennel Cough: If you board your dog, go to the dog park, compete in performance events, go to training classes, take your doodle to the groomer, etc., your veterinarian may recommend the combined vaccine for Canine Parainfluenza Virus and *Bordetella bronchiseptica*. This is an intranasal vaccine that is given up to every 6 months. It has few side effects and is considered relatively safe. Proof of the vaccination is often required by boarding kennels, training clubs, and groomers.

Canine Influenza Virus (CIV): In the early 2000s, racing greyhounds in Florida developed CIV, a serious, sometimes life-threatening, upper respiratory disease. Areas at greatest risk for CIV include Florida as well as Colorado, Pennsylvania, New Jersey, and New York. If you and your doodle live in these areas, travel to them, or are in areas that dogs from these areas come to, your veterinarian may recommend this vaccine.

Canine *Leptospira*: There are many different strains of *Leptospira*, which makes creating a vaccine to protect dogs from exposure more difficult. The current vaccine provides protection from an estimated 50 to 75 percent of the existing known strains. Dogs are more likely to be exposed to Leptospirosis if they have contact with livestock, live in rural areas, and/or live in areas frequented by wild mammals. A "Lepto" infection can be fatal and has a high morbidity rate, and it can be passed to humans. The vaccine has a high rate of anaphylactic reactions in dogs. It is hoped that advances in vaccines may decrease the likelihood of severe reactions in the future; however, currently, it is a vaccine that requires a careful risk-benefit analysis before administering it to your doodle.

Lyme Vaccine: The canine *Borrelia burgdorferi* (Lyme) vaccine is one that requires a serious risk-benefit analysis before vaccinating your pup. Lyme disease is endemic in the East Coast of the U.S., and this is one area of the country where the risk of contracting Lyme disease may far outweigh any adverse reactions to the vaccine. Topical products can be used, in addition to the vaccine, to prevent tick exposure. If a dog contracts Lyme disease and *if* it is diagnosed quickly, the dog can be treated with relative success with antimicrobials.

CONTROLLING PARASITES

When your pup is at his first wellness check, his stool sample will be examined for the presence of worms. As noted previously, *don't panic* if he has worms. This is not uncommon. A couple types of worms can be passed to the puppy through the mother, even though the adult worms were not present in the mother. (See "Roundworms," below.) Usually, the breeder will have already dewormed the puppies at the age of 2 weeks. A second deworming is typically performed at 12 weeks, if the puppy's stool indicates he still has worms.

Roundworms These parasitic worms are frequently passed down from mother to pups as the encysted larvae in the mother are impervious

Preventing Reinfection

Pick up and dispose of all puppy stools immediately.

Do not allow healthy pets (as well as children!) to enter the area where the puppy, who is being dewormed, is defecating.

to dewormers and can remain inactive in the female dog's body for years before they activate and begin migrating. Larvae can migrate to the uterus to infect the unborn pups, or they can migrate in the nursing mother to the mammary gland and the puppies can become infected through their mother's milk. This worm can be passed to humans.

Hookworms An infestation of hookworms can grow to such size as to kill your puppy. Puppies can ingest contaminated water or contaminated matter containing hookworm larvae. Puppies can also become infected from their mother's milk. This infection can be passed to humans, too.

Tapeworms Dogs usually become infected with tapeworms by ingesting fleas that have tapeworm eggs in them or by ingesting rabbits or birds. Yes. Disgusting, but it happens. Your doodle, if infected, can pass this to humans.

Whipworms Whipworm eggs can live in the environment for months to years. Once ingested, they become active and develop into worms. So just when you think you've got everything under control, if your doodle ingests soil, water, or other matter that contains embryonated eggs, he will have a whipworm infestation again.

Heartworms This deadly worm is *not* transmitted through fecal matter; rather, it is transmitted through a unique lifecycle. When an adult female heartworm is present in a dog, fox, coyote, or wolf, it produces microfilaria that circulate in the infected animal's bloodstream.

If a mosquito bites an infected dog, fox, coyote, or wolf, it picks up the microfilaria, or microscopic juvenile worms, of the heartworm. In the mosquito, the microfilaria mature and develop into infective stage larvae. When the infected mosquito bites *another* dog (or susceptible wild animal), the infective larvae enter the surface of the animal's skin through the mosquito's bite wound. Once inside the new host, the larvae mature into adult heartworms within 6 months. Mature heartworms can live up to 7 years in dogs, with female heartworms producing microfilaria that circulate in the infected dog's bloodstream.

Heartworm disease can cause a dog to develop heart failure over time, and large numbers of heartworms can develop sudden blockages of blood flow within the heart, leading to cardiovascular collapse, or "caval syndrome." In less severe cases, a dog can be treated; however, the treatment is not simple nor is it without its risks.

Heartworm is one of the simplest worm infestations to prevent. Preventives are available as a once-a-month chewable, a once-a-month topical, or a twice-a-year injection. Heartworm preventives are also effective in preventing several intestinal worm infestations and/or flea and tick infestations.

Flea Product Caution

Never use a flea product on a puppy unless your veterinarian has approved the product.

Check with your veterinarian on the different types of heartworm preventives that are available for your doodle. Make sure to keep your doodle protected year-round.

Fleas An "outside" parasitic pest, fleas can wreak havoc on your doodle, causing intense itching as well as flea allergy dermatitis that can manifest as ugly, infected hotspots. Fleas can also spread infestations of tapeworms, as well as transmit several serious diseases, such as Plague, *Bartonella*, and *Rickettsia* infections.

Fleas can also take over your home. Eggs can fall from the dog's coat into the dog's bedding as well as your couches, beds, and carpets. If the temperatures are warm and humid, the eggs hatch and larvae emerge. Fleas also go through a pupae stage and only emerge as adult fleas when a suitable host is located, such as your doodle lying on his bed.

To stop the cycle requires a multipronged approach:

✔ Treat the adult fleas living on your doodle by using shampoos, sprays, dips, or topical medications. (An oral pill is also available to kill adult fleas within hours.)

✔ Vacuum all areas of your home regularly and repeatedly with a quality vacuum using a HEPA filtered bag.

✔ After each vacuuming, remove the vacuum bag, seal it in a plastic bag, and dispose of it immediately.

✔ Wash all bedding in hot, soapy water or on a sanitary cycle in your washing machine to remove eggs and pupae.

✔ Discuss with your veterinarian additional ways to prevent fleas from taking up residence on your doodle again.

Ticks Ticks, like fleas, carry a plethora of diseases: Lyme disease, *Bartonella*, Erlichiosis, *Rickettsia*, and Meningoencephalitis. Fortunately, many of the same preventives that work for fleas also work for ticks. Additionally, it is advisable to hand check your doodle for ticks on a regular basis. If you find a tick, use tweezers, firmly grab the tick as close as possible to the dog's skin, and

slowly pull the tick out. Be careful not to pull so quickly as to allow the head to remain in the dog's skin. If that happens, try to tweeze it out. If that's not possible, watch the area and soak it in hot, salty water to encourage the removal of the head. If you find a deer tick on your dog, bag the tick and take it to your veterinarian to have it tested for Lyme disease.

Mites Among the world of mites, there are several types that can plague dogs. *Otedectes cynotis*, or ear mites, are found in a dog's ears. If you notice your doodle shaking his head, scratching a lot, and generally being bothered, it could be ear mites. Ear mites are very contagious and can spread rapidly from your dog's ears to other parts of his body and to other dogs. The ear mite can cause your dog to scratch so violently as to damage his ear canal, or create hematomas that, when he shakes his head, burst blood everywhere. Treatment for ear mites is an ear cleaner that is used for 7–10 days and then repeated 2 weeks later.

The other two types of mites cause mange. One mite lives deep in the hair follicles, and the other lives just under the surface of the skin. Both forms are treated using a topical medication. More serious infestations may require more aggressive treatment using special shampoos and dips, along with an oral medication. If you suspect your doodle has mites, consult with your veterinarian immediately for the safest and most efficient way of returning your doodle to a healthy state.

Giardia *Giardia* is a parasite that can be found in streams, rivers, and other bodies of fresh water; however, dogs with *giardia* can shed the cysts in their stools. So, the most common source of *giardia* is in infected water; infected surfaces (crowded kennels with a dog that has *giardia*) or common areas frequented by dogs (parks, play areas, etc.) can also be a source of infection for your pup. Puppies with *giardia* can become seriously ill in a very short amount of time. A puppy from a clean environment should not have *giardia;* however, if he is in a situation where adult dogs have the parasite and are not being treated, he can be exposed to the parasite. Symptoms include vomiting and diarrhea that is often light in color, foul smelling, and containing mucus. The parasite can be treated with medications. The *giardia* vaccination has been proven *not* to be effective in either treating the infestation or preventing an infestation. The vaccination is sometimes used in kennel settings to limit shedding of the parasite by infected dogs (and, therefore, reduce the probability of new dogs and puppies becoming infected).

THE SPAY/NEUTER QUESTION

Often, Labradoodles and Australian Labradoodles will be spayed or neutered while with the breeder, and you will not have to worry about this. If your puppy is intact, your veterinarian will discuss with you about your plans to alter your doodle. Altering your doodle spares you from a lot of headaches. Dogs will often come into sexual maturity anywhere between 7 and 9 months of age, but sometimes sooner. Once a dog reaches sexual maturity, the female will come into season (it's messy, requires crating, and can last as long as a month) and male dogs will begin marking their territory and will be capable of impregnating an intact female in season.

Health reasons for altering your doodle include eliminating the chance of uterine or mammary cancer in females and eliminating the chance of testicular cancer in males, as well as reducing the chance of death by being hit by a car—a true possibility for a young, virile, athletic male getting loose in search of a mate.

Spay/neuter is a very routine surgery for veterinarians, and the younger the pup, the faster the recovery time. Your doodle may have to wear an Elizabethan collar that prevents the pup from licking or pulling at his stitches until they can be removed; however, your greatest problem will be keeping your puppy calm the second day after surgery. They often act as if nothing has happened.

IDENTIFICATION FOR YOUR LABRADOODLE

You already have your puppy's ID tags made and you've attached the tag to his collar and maybe another one to his harness as well. But what if he gets loose and loses his collar? Or, what if the tag catches and pulls off his harness? A permanent form of identification will help return your beloved Labradoodle or Australian Labradoodle to you.

Tattoos: When your puppy is getting spayed or neutered, this would be a good time to tattoo your doodle with a unique number that can be registered for a fee with the National Dog Registry (NDR). The benefit of the tattoo is that shelters, veterinary clinics, animal control authorities, and animal laboratories are supposed to check the inner thigh area of a dog to see if he has an identifying tattoo. If a tattoo is discovered, most facilities will make a serious effort to track the tattoo

and contact the owner. The downside of the tattoo is that hair can grow over the tattoo area and it can be difficult to spot.

Microchips: This form of identification is no bigger than a grain of rice and is imbedded under your doodle's skin, in between his shoulder blades. Each microchip has a unique number that shows up on a handheld scanner. The scanner is used by all shelters and most veterinarians. The procedure to insert the microchip does not require anesthesia. When receiving a microchip for your dog, make sure that the chip that is being used is scannable by a universal scanner, and that it does not require a proprietary scanner.

Doodle Health

The health of any dog is directly proportional to what each parent carries genetically, and whether the parents are carriers of certain otherwise "hidden" diseases. So, where does that leave the Labradoodle and the Australian Labradoodle?

For the Labradoodle, the Labrador parent, at a minimum, should have been cleared of hip dysplasia, elbow dysplasia, and certain eye diseases. The standard poodle parent should also be cleared of hip dysplasia and eye diseases, as well as sebaceous adenitis (a difficult skin condition to treat).

For the F2, F1B, and all early generations of the Labradoodle, the parents should at a minimum be tested and clear of hip dysplasia, as well as any eye diseases, as tested through an annual eye exam. Note, this eye exam is not your everyday eye exam; it is one that is performed by a veterinary ophthalmologist (see "Disorders of the Eye," page 71).

The Australian Labradoodle breed clubs recommend that, at a minimum, breeding ALs are tested and cleared of hip and elbow dysplasia, and have a current eye exam by a veterinary ophthalmologist that shows the dogs are clear of disease. In addition, the AL breed clubs encourage additional genetic testing for those diseases that can be discovered

Who Performs Genetic Testing?

Currently there are two companies that are approved by the ALAA for genetic testing, and those include VetGen (*www.vetgen.com*) and Pawprints Genetics (*www.pawprintsgenetics.com*). The ALCA requires testing from OptiGen (*www.optigen.com*). Additionally, DDC Veterinary (*www.vetdnacenter.com*) provides testing for all genetic diseases of the Labradoodle and Australian Labradoodle.

DNA Testing

The DNA testing that was used to register dogs with ALAA and ALCA requires a cheek swab. From this cheek swab sample, the testing facility determines the dog's unique genetic profile that can be used to identify that individual doodle, and can be used to verify breeding using this doodle. This DNA test is different from genetic testing for hereditary diseases (a blood sample), and can only be used for dog identification, not isolating diseases.

(clear, carrier, or with the disease) through DNA testing.

The following information on diseases, conditions, and injuries of the Labradoodle and Australian Labradoodle is arranged by the area of the body the disease or condition affects. For now, health concerns are based on the health concerns of the breeds involved in developing the Labradoodle, as mentioned above, as well as those conditions that breeders have determined are areas of concern.

In the health conditions listed below, in addition to basic information on each disease, it is also noted where the concern comes from (Labrador, Poodle, Cocker, etc.), how common this health concern occurs, what the treatment for the disease or condition is, and if there is a genetic test available.

STARTING WITH SKIN

Atopic Allergic Dermatitis

With 15 percent of Labradors suffering from atopic allergic dermatitis and Poodles also notably allergic to multiple airborne and food allergens, the Labradoodle is at risk for atopic allergic dermatitis. Food allergens are usually determined by restricting the dog's food to an allergen-free diet for 6 weeks, and then gradually adding specific foods back into the diet to determine the cause of the allergy. In the case of airborne allergens, determining the cause can be a bit more difficult: Airborne allergens are ingested when the allergens (e.g., pollens, mold spurs, and dust mites) settle on a surface over which a doodle walks, and then the doodle licks his paws, ingesting the allergens.

Symptoms of atopic allergic dermatitis include red, itchy inflamed skin, caused by the ingestion of either airborne allergens (e.g., mold, dust, pollen) or foods. Inflamed and infected ears may also signal an allergic reaction. Treatments for airborne allergens include frequent bathing of the doodle to minimize ingestion of allergens, and medications such as corticosteroids, antihistamines, topical sprays, and cyclosporine (in long-term cases). Also, hyposensitization therapy has been helpful in some atopic allergic dermati-

tis cases, in which injections of allergens are given over a 6- to 12-month period.

Contact Dermatitis

With this type of allergy, the dog must come in contact with an allergen to cause the allergic reaction. Contact dermatitis could occur after the topical application of a flea and tick medication, for example, or perhaps a soap used to wash his bedding that comes in contact with an area with little hair, such as the abdomen, groin, or feet. Treatment includes bathing the doodle to remove the allergen and isolating the allergen and preventing the doodle from coming in contact with it again. In acute cases, corticosteroids and antihistamines may be used.

Hot Spot, Summer Sore, Moist Eczema

This skin condition is a bacterial infection that can have a variety of causes but often stems from a response to an airborne allergen, an allergy to flea bites, an injury, or sometimes even boredom. Hot spots occur most frequently in the summer months when the weather is warm and humid. A hot spot will appear as a circular, red, and moist area of skin that has thinning hair. The hot spot can grow quickly if not treated. Treatment for a hot spot involves surgical shaving of the area by a veterinarian to expose the area to air and help dry it out. Then, the area is cleaned, patted dry, and treated with hydrocortisone spray or cream.

Pyoderma

This is a skin condition that can occur in any breed but is more common in Labradors.

Pyoderma is a bacterial infection of the skin and causes itchiness, pustules, crusted skin, small raised lesions, hair loss, and a dried discharge. Treatment includes topical medications and oral antibiotics. Depending on the location of the infection, a doodle may have to wear an Elizabethan collar (cone of shame).

Lipomas

These are the fatty tumors that appear under the skin that are benign and tend to appear in geriatric dogs. It is always a good idea to have these tumors tested to make sure they are not cancerous; however, if they are lipomas, they are rarely removed unless one grows to a size that makes it difficult for your doodle to move or lie down comfortably.

Sebaceous Adenitis

This is, fortunately, a rare condition, but sebaceous adenitis (SA) is an inherited allergy that affects the hair follicles and lubrication of the skin. Labradoodles most likely inherited SA from Standard Poodles (which are most highly affected by SA), but crosses with Toy and Miniature Poodles afflicted with SA also could have contributed to the problem. SA can be "subclinical." In other words, the disease is present but the dog shows no outward signs of the disease. Dogs actively suffering from SA will have scaly, flaky, or peeling skin in areas of hair loss, odors, sores, and even secondary infections. SA does not have a cure, but it can be treated. Treatments for SA may include prednisone, tetracycline, and mineral oil soaks, as well as bathing with a medicated shampoo three times a week.

Currently there is no DNA test to detect SA; however, diagnosis can be made with a skin punch test or biopsy.

MOVING TO MUSCULAR AND JOINT DISORDERS

Osteoarthritis

Larger breeds, as they age, are susceptible to chronic joint inflammation caused by the deterioration of the joint cartilage. Overweight dogs are also at increased risk of developing osteoarthritis.

Prevention, by keeping your Labradoodle fit and at an appropriate weight, will help.

Testing Is an Investment

Having a dog's hips and elbows x-rayed and then read by an approved radiologist in order to receive hip and elbow ratings, having an annual eye exam performed by a board-certified veterinary ophthalmologist, having a cardiac exam performed (also by a veterinary specialist), and having a test for Subaceous Adenitis (SA) every 2 years will cost more than $1,000 *per dog*. Add to this a complete genetic panel for primary diseases, as well as a supplementary panel test for less common diseases in the breed's lines, breeders will incur costs well over $2,000 per dog. If a breeder is performing these tests and is using them to prevent carriers of disease from running in their lines, they are able to produce a healthier dog. To them it is worth every penny.

Most elderly dogs, however, do develop this condition. Treatments can include nutraceuticals, such as joint supplements (glucosamine, chondroitin, MSM, green-lipped mussel, and other chondroprotective substances); mild, gentle, and regular exercise ("motion is lotion"); the use of a newer form of treatment—the Class IV therapeutic laser, which stimulates blood flow to tissues and may greatly improve arthritic conditions; Adequin injections (a lubricating substance that is injected into the arthritic joint capsule and is thought to encourage the production of cartilage); well tolerated pain medications, such as Tramadol; and, finally, medications such as those from the canine NSAID family, which include Rimadyl, EtoGesic, Deramaxx, Previcox, Metacam, and Feldene. NSAIDs are usually prescribed with caution as Labradors, and thus Labradoodles, can have serious side effects to these medications.

Cruciate Ligament Rupture

This injury is comparable to a torn knee ligament. The rupture causes partial to complete instability of the dog's stifle joint in the rear leg. Surgery to repair this injury is costly (usually more than $3,000). Labradors have a higher incidence of this injury than other purebreds; a recent study also indicated that mixed breeds have a higher propensity to this injury than all purebreds.

Elbow Dysplasia

The term "elbow dysplasia" is a generalized term for a debilitating condition of the elbow joint that has multiple causes, of which a combination of up to three different joint abnormalities may be present. Certain breeds tend to be afflicted with this condition. The Labradoodle's parent, the Labrador Retriever, is a breed that is over-represented for elbow dysplasia, making the Labradoodle at increased risk. Treatments are surgical (depending on the cause of the ED), expensive, and not always successful. At the current time, there is no genetic test to predetermine the condition. Elbow dysplasia (as well as the absence of ED) is diagnosed through X-rays and certifying agencies, such as the Orthopedic Foundation for Animals (OFA), which rates the condition of a dog's elbows at the age of 24 months or older. Elbows are rated as "normal," or free of disease; or if disease is present, graded from 1 (least abnormal) to 3 (most abnormal).

Screening for ED is required for all Australian Labradoodles to be used for breeding by ALAA and ALCA breeders.

Canine Hip Dysplasia (CHD)

CHD, unfortunately, is the most commonly inherited orthopedic disease in all dogs. It afflicts millions of dogs each year. A young dog (under age 1) may develop CHD after an injury to his hip joint that causes the ball of the femur to misalign with the pelvic socket. Usually, however, most dogs are born with a femoral head and pelvic socket laxity that causes the progression of CHD. The ill-fitting femur and pelvic socket causes a destructive cycle of fracturing, rough healing (healing with a rough, instead of smooth, surface), more fracturing, and more rough healing until there is disfiguration of not only the femur ball but the pelvic socket, too. The disease causes severe pain and inflammation.

In mild cases of CHD, the same treatments used for osteoarthritis (e.g., weight management, hip and joint supplements, anti-inflammatory drugs, and pain medications) can be helpful. In more serious cases, surgery may be required. Depending on the surgery, costs may range from $2,000 to more than $4,500.

Diagnosis, and screening for disease, is performed through X-rays, which are read by radiologists for one of the organizations performing this service, (e.g., OFA, eVet Diagnostics [*www.evetdiagnostics.com*], Australian Veterinary Association [AVA at *www.ava.com*], or PennHip [*www.info. antechimagingservices.com/pennhip*]).

DISORDERS OF THE EYE

Australian Labradoodle breeders belonging to the ALAA or the ALCA are encouraged to have each of their breeding dogs examined by a member of the American College of Veterinary Ophthalmologists (ACVO) and pronounced clear of disease before the dog is used in a breeding program. Labradoodle breeders should also have this ophthalmic test performed on their breeding dogs as well. The eye exam given by the ACVO tests for clinical signs of many debilitating eye diseases that frequently result in blindness and for which there is definite evidence of heritability in one or more breeds.

Nuclear Sclerosis

This eye condition is the hallmark of an aging dog. It is a normal change that creates

a slight graying of the lens. It usually appears in both eyes at the same time. It is not painful, and it does not limit the vision of the dog as much as you might think. There is no treatment for this condition; however, if you see this clouding occurring, even if your dog is older, you should have your doodle's eyes checked by a veterinarian as soon as possible, to rule out a more serious condition.

Cataracts

Canine cataracts can develop from disease (diabetes), old age, and trauma. Cataracts, however, can also develop as an inherited condition. Heritable cataracts may be present at birth or develop when the dog is young (1–3 years old). If your doodle is diagnosed with a cataract, he may have minor vision problems (if the cataract is small) or he could become blind quite rapidly as the cataract covers the entire lens. The only way to treat cataracts is through surgery, which involves replacing the

lens with an artificial lens and can average between $1,500 and $3,000 per eye.

Retinal Dysplasia

This eye condition is a malformation of a doodle's retina and occurs when two layers of the retina do not form together properly, creating folds (mild case), larger areas of defective retinal development (moderate), and in severe cases the retinal layers do not come together at all and cause retinal detachment and blindness. Puppies are born with whatever level of retinal dysplasia they will have; the condition does not regress. Even at the mild level, the doodle will have vision loss, as the folds on the retina will create blind spots in his vision.

Retinal dysplasia can be detected as early as 6–8 weeks; however, because of how small a doodle's eye is at this age (and they are wriggling a lot), the condition is easier to see with a veterinary ophthalmic exam when the puppy is 6 months old. The condition is largely hereditary; however, there are prenatal infections, such as herpes virus and parvovirus, that can cause the condition independent of genetics.

Labrador Retrievers have such a high incidence of this hereditary condition that breeding is not recommended at *any* level (even mild). Additionally, this eye condition is thought to be linked to a second hereditary disease, Achondroplasia, a form of dwarfism in which the forelimbs to not grow to a normal size. Though relatively rare in Labs, Achondroplasia has been directly linked to the presence of retinal folds.

This hereditary condition has a DNA test available.

Macular Corneal Dystrophy (MCD)

This eye disease is hereditary and commonly affects middle-aged Labradors. It is not painful; however, it is progressive, in that it makes the affected dog's vision increasingly limited. The disease presents itself as cloudiness in the cornea. The only treatment for the disease in humans is a corneal transplant, but this surgery is not yet available for dogs. This condition is relatively rare, and a DNA test is available for this hereditary disease.

Progressive Retinal Atrophy (PRA)

PRA, also known as progressive retinal degeneration (PRD), refers to a group of diseases that are hereditary and cause blindness. PRA causes a slow, progressive degeneration (or death) of the retinal tissue in the eye. PRA is inherited; however, it is inherited in different ways in different breeds. In some breeds' variations, blindness develops at different ages and with different progression rates. PRA has been seen in virtually every registered breed and in mixed breeds as well. The Labradoodle's parent, the Labrador, is affected by central PRA, which causes the loss of night vision first and can progress to total blindness. An early sign of this disease is what some people describe as an "abnormal shine" in the dog's eyes, caused by the inability of the pupil to constrict properly. In other forms of PRA, there are very few early signs that the dog is having difficulties.

Cocker Spaniels (present in the Australian Labradoodle's bloodlines) and Miniature Poodles are afflicted with rod-cone degeneration, which is slightly different. Symptoms for the Cocker are not apparent until the dog is 2–7 years old; a Poodle may display the disorder as young as 6 months to 5 years.

DNA testing is available for three types of PRD.

OTHER DISEASES

None of the diseases in this section are very common; however, they do appear in Labradoodles and Australian Labradoodles—and the breeds involved in developing both the Labradoodle and AL—so, when a breeder has his or her breeding stock DNA tested for these hereditary diseases, it is definitely a plus for the puppy buyer. All of the following diseases and conditions have DNA testing available.

Addison's Disease

Also known as Hypoadrenocorticism, Addison's disease is a hereditary condition that results from an adrenal gland that is not producing enough hormones (glucocorticoids and mineralocorticoids), causing weakness, dehydration, depression, low blood pressure, thirst, shaking, hair loss, vomiting, and weight loss. The disease can be life-threatening in acute episodes; treatment for chronic cases requires supplementing the deficient hormone (as injections) for life. The disease is relatively rare, but it presents itself more in young to middle-aged female dogs and has been linked with Standard Poodles and Soft-Coated Wheaten Terriers—thus the link to Labradoodles and Australian Labradoodles.

Degenerative Myelopathy

This hereditary disease progressively robs a dog of his mobility, beginning with weakness in the dog's hind limbs, difficulty rising, knuckling over of the toes, muscle loss, and tremors in the rear legs. The early stages of this disease usually appear after 8 years or more. As the disease progresses, the dog eventually suffers front leg weakness, urinary and fecal incontinence, and organ failure leading to eventual death. There is no cure, and the prognosis for dogs with the disease is poor, with most dogs being euthanized within 6 months to 3 years after diagnosis. Degenerative Myelopathy has been detected in 124 breeds and is reported to appear with a 7 percent frequency in Labs.

Exercise Induced Collapse (EIC)

This disease was first diagnosed in Labrador Retrievers but has now been identified in a number of breeds. EIC is a recessively inherited condition, which results in hind limb weakness after relatively short but intense periods of extreme exercise. Symptoms can be seen in dogs as young as 5 months to 3 years old. Treatment includes avoiding the activities that typically cause the dog to collapse, and halting activity at the first sign of the dog showing physical weakness. In addition, owners can give the dog water do drink, or spray him with cool water to help lower his body temperature.

Hereditary Nasal Parakeratosis (HNPK)

This hereditary disease found in Labradors, and present in the genetics of Labradoodles and ALs, causes a thickening of the skin on the dog's nose. The outer layer of skin produces too much keratin, and the excess skin becomes hard, thick, dried out, callous-like, and can develop cracks, which can become infected. Generally, the condition occurs in the first year of a dog's life. There is no cure for HNPK but there are treatments available to ease the symptoms, which include regular veterinary appointments to trim and cut away the excess keratin. Other treatments could include wet wraps, soaks in propylene glycol, and other topical solutions.

Von Willebrand's Disease Type 1 (vWD1)

vWD1 is a bleeding disorder that can cause bruising and frequent nose bleeds, and when puppy teeth are lost, the dogs with vWD1 will bleed from the mouth. The inability to properly form blood clots comes from an abnormally low level of von Willebrand coagulation factor (vWf), the protein that is essential for normal blood clotting. The severity of the disease ranges, with some dogs not being diagnosed until they have surgery (such as a spay or neuter) and excessive bleeding is noticed. Dogs with the disease usually can live a normal life, if precautions are taken.

THE "C" WORD

Unfortunately, there is not a DNA test (yet) for cancer. And, according to a recent statistic published by a pet insurance company of claims made in the past year, mixed breeds had the highest rate of cancer (over all purebred breeds) and made up 20 percent of all dogs with cancer. This was followed by

Poodles (#4) and Labradors (in the top 10 to 12, depending on the study).

Cancers common to the Labrador include malignant lymphomas (blood cancers) and mast cell tumors (tumors that cause allergic responses, gastric ulcers, and internal bleeding). Both Poodles and Labradors are more susceptible to insulinomas (malignant tumors of the pancreas). Additionally, Standard Poodles have a higher susceptibility to squamous cell carcinoma, a form of skin cancer. Dark pigmented Labs (black Labs) and black Poodles are more susceptible to canine melanomas. If found in the mouth (oral melanoma), it is a particularly aggressive malignant tumor. Mammary cancer (breast cancer) is reported to make up 50 percent of all tumors in female dogs, with unspayed dogs more likely to develop tumors, of which half are malignant. This is one cancer that can be prevented with timely spaying (before the first or second heat cycle).

Signs of Cancer

The National Canine Cancer Foundation (*www.wearethecure.org*) published the 10 early warning signs that you cannot ignore as a dog owner and must keep a wary eye out that something could be seriously wrong with your dog. The ten warning signs are as follows:

1. Abnormal swellings that persist or continue to grow
2. Sores that don't heal
3. Weight loss
4. Loss of appetite
5. Bleeding or discharge from any body opening
6. Offensive odor
7. Difficulty eating or swallowing
8. Hesitation to exercise or loss of stamina
9. Persistent lameness or stiffness
10. Difficulty breathing, urinating, or defecating

Most importantly, trust your "gut" feeling. You know your doodle better than anyone else, and if you think something is "off" with him, you are probably right. If it is cancer, your doodle's best chance of survival is to get a diagnosis as soon as possible and decide on a treatment plan. Depending on the cancer type, treatment plans may range from surgery, chemotherapy, radiation therapy, medication, and palliative care. Your veterinarian will help you make the best choice for you and your dog.

Training Basics

Training your Labradoodle or Australian Labradoodle from the moment you get him benefits you and him in many, many ways.

Lack of training is perhaps the greatest reason for a Labradoodle or an Australian Labradoodle to fail in a home. Too many Labradoodle owners think that somehow the doodle puppy automatically, and with no intervention from them, will grow into the amazing adult dog that they've read about and seen all over the Internet. The doodle did not get there on his own. Behind every "perfect" adult dog is a lot of time, effort, patience, and dedication by the owner.

BENEFITS OF TRAINING YOUR DOODLE

Training your doodle works. Even if you've never trained a dog before, if you work hard to understand how to train him and work with him every day, he will be trained!

The act of training establishes leadership in a fun, gentle way. Labradoodles and Australian Labradoodles are not dominant breeds by nature, but any breed, without knowing who the boss is, will take over that position if a human isn't already filling the job. You do not want to live by your dog's rules. Once your doodle has elevated himself to the position of house leader, it takes a lot of work and patience to restore the natural order of things; often, this requires professional intervention to not only retrain the dog, but to retrain yourself as well. It's easier to establish yourself as the leader by having your dog *sit* or *down* on command several times a day.

Training provides your doodle with the mental stimulation and interaction with you that he craves. Yes, exercise will help to settle your doodle and it does provide another source of interaction with you, but training makes him think, problem solve, and get rewarded for his efforts. It has been said that the greatest crime against a doodle is to not stimulate that big brain of his.

As is true with any dog, when you spend time each day training your dog, you will foster a relationship that it is hard to describe in words. You will feel it. You will know that your doodle loves you and the depth of that love is unfathomable. It is worth every second and will provide you with a canine companion relationship that few other dog owners ever experience.

It is so fun to live with a well-trained dog. You will be able to take your doodle virtually anywhere that allows dogs, and he will behave like a prince. He won't drag you so you will want to take him on walks. He can perform tricks to amuse children. He will politely wait for pats from the elderly. You can have friends and family over and he will accept strangers into the home with such grace that you will never have to "put the dog up."

If having such a well-trained dog seems impossible, it's not. You can do this! Ready to get started?

Physical Praise

Did you know the greatest reward to a dog is a physical reward, such as patting and rubbing him while you are telling him what a bright and beautiful and good boy he is?

POSITIVE, REWARD-BASED TRAINING THEORY (AND PRACTICE)

Positive, reward-based training has been in place for more than a decade now and is the accepted way to train puppies and adult dogs. The most important concepts of this training are:

1. Behaviors are shaped using lures to position the dog.
2. Rewards (treats, praise, physical pats, and love) are given for correct behaviors.
3. Dogs are set up for success, with virtually no chance of failing.

So, this is how this works. For the *sit*, you will use a treat to lure your dog from a standing position into a *sit*. Once the dog is in the *sit*, you reward him with your voice and pats and with the treat that is being used as a lure. The action of *sitting* is then reinforced through repetition and more rewards (which don't always have to be treats!).

Setting your dog up for success is also important with reward-based training as the more correct repetitions a dog has of an exercise, the faster he learns. To set up your dog for success, you will withhold teaching him the verbal command of a behavior until he can produce the behavior consistently.

So with the *sit* command as an example, you won't link the command "*Sit!*" with the behavior, until he sits every time you pull out the treat and move it from his nose to between his ears. Once he is luring into the *sit* without fail, then link the command "*Sit*" with the final *action of sitting*. So, you will say "*Sit*" as he finishes folding into the *sit*. In this way, he associates the word, "*Sit*," not with a crouch or with a stand but with the action of sitting.

Using Training Treats to Shape Behaviors

Who knew that using a tiny piece of food could get even the biggest Labradoodle to fold into a *sit*, or lie into a *down*? It's pretty amazing, but using lures as treats works, and it's easy to do if you follow a few rules.

Rule 1: The doodle gets the treat *only* when he has achieved something. Your doodle does not get treats for free anymore. He has to do something, and when he is learning a new skill or a new command, he has to put forth an effort. You can, however, reward efforts toward the end goal. For example, if you're working on getting your doodle to shift from a *sit* into a *down*, you can treat him if he makes progress and starts to come to the floor. His next reward can come when he gets a little farther down. And, of course, when he learns to drop it all the way to the floor, he gets a jackpot (several treats).

Rule 2: Verbal commands are only linked when the doodle is certain to provide the behavior. So, the reason why you can reward your dog for making headway into learning a new behavior is that you have

not told him what the behavior is. There is no chance that he will learn that *sit* means "squat," as you have not linked the command "*Sit!*" with any behavior yet. When he is consistently rolling back into that *sit*, then you link the verbal command "*Sit!*" as he finishes his *sit*. The better he gets, the sooner you can give the command.

Rule 3: Do not repeat commands. He heard you. If he doesn't provide the behavior that he is supposed to, that means he's confused. You must not repeat the command; if you repeat the command, you've just taught him that he sits after you say "*Sit!*" twice. Grab a lure, and lure him into a *sit*. This is called taking a step back. You will learn to do this whenever your doodle gets confused, and this usually occurs because you're moving too fast (he hasn't had enough solid repetitions to cement his learning), or there are additional factors that are challenging him, such as a new environment or distractions, or he's at the end of the training session and he's gotten tired and is losing focus—which brings us to the next rule . . .

Rule 4: Keep it fun. Little puppies have a short attention span, and they tire pretty easily. So, short, quick sessions, no more than 5–10 minutes but sprinkled throughout the day, will work best with your puppy. Older puppies still benefit from quick training sessions throughout the day (every moment can be a learning moment), but the older they get, the longer you can work with them. Usually 20–30 minutes is a good time period for a more formal training session; however, don't give up those all day learning moments!

Whatever length of time you set for training, your goal must always be to stop your training session before your doodle stops. Quit while he is still having fun. If he tires, his mind will wander, it will be harder to get his attention, and then he will be slower in responding to you. If you hit this point and realize it too late, pick an *easy* task for your doodle to perform and quit on a high note.

Also, never train when you're angry, exhausted, stressed, or impatient. Your doodle will pick up on this, as your leash is like a lightning rod back to your doodle. He won't know why you are so out of sorts, but it will affect how he responds to you.

Rule 5: Train Hungry. Okay, so there is one more secret to all this. Train when those treats you have in your pocket mean a lot to your puppy. Do not train immediately after a meal. Even a chow hound will be slow to respond when his belly is full. If you can, train before meals. And make sure your treats are what he would consider a high-value food treat.

Good choices are chopped up tiny bits of cooked chicken breast; microwaved, low-sodium hot dogs (they get chewy and a paper towel under the treats wicks away the grease); as well as any of the all-natural training treats.

HOW TO SET UP YOUR DOODLE FOR SUCCESS

A really big component of training your doodle successfully is learning to be patient and taking small steps. The small progress you are making with each successive movement toward accomplishing a behavior is setting up your puppy to succeed. So, be patient, move slowly, and confirm what your doodle has learned with repetition.

Repetition

As you teach your dog a skill, he needs to successfully provide that behavior on a regular basis before you make the skill more difficult. A general rule to follow is that if your doodle gives you a speedy, confident, and correct response eight out of ten times, then you can add a new degree of difficulty.

Attention!

Before you give a command, you should always have your doodle's complete attention. This means you have to be more interesting than anything else. It is also why trainers frequently train with a dog's name as the attention cue, so, now they will say, "Baxter!" (they now have his attention), "*Sit!*" and he sits.

To train a dog with his name as an attention cue is simple. Say his name when he is nearby, and praise him ("*Good boy!*") as soon as he makes eye contact, then treat him. Repeat. Praise and treat. Do this every time, and he will be all eyes on you when you say his name.

Going Backward Before Moving Forward

When making an exercise more difficult, you want to add only one new element or degree of difficulty at a time. But, to make sure he succeeds at this new level, you need to take his training back one step. Let's say your puppy is very good at sitting quickly on command in your kitchen, where it is only you and him. Now, you'd like to have him sit on command when he is at the big box store for pets, so people can pet him. What do you do?

If you go to the pet store, and give him the command to *sit*, it is very likely that he is far too excited and distracted to obey your command. What do you do next? Most normal humans get frustrated and say "*Sit!*" again, but louder. No response. Then, "*Sit! SIT! SIT!!!!!*" And, he still isn't sitting. You're embarrassed (get used to it; dogs are humbling creatures for the best of trainers), and now you don't know what to do.

When you add a layer of complexity to your puppy's training, take his training a step back. Make it so he can't fail. In this case, when you are in the pet store do the following:

- Take him to a quiet place in the store.
- Pull out your treat and get his attention on *you*.
- Use the treat to mold him into a *sit*.
- Treat and praise him.
- Repeat.
- When he is sitting regularly with the treat and only then, start adding back in the verbal command, still using the treat. Get him solid on this.
- Then, move to a slightly busier section of the store. Start from the beginning again by using a treat to mold him into a *sit*.

Gradually, you will be able to ask for a *sit* when someone is nearby. If he does not *sit* at any point, be prepared to start from the beginning again, and build him back up.

Environment

A change in environment can mean going to a new place, or adding a distraction in an "old" place. With all new command training, start in a distraction-free place. Then, as he is solid in a distraction-free environment, add new distractions to challenge him, such as a toy on the floor or a person sitting quietly in the room, and make the exercise progressively more difficult. Remember, though, to go back in the exercise (make it easier) before you go forward with the new distraction.

Distance

Distance comes into play mostly when teaching the *sit-stay* or *down-stay* commands, and the *come* command. When adding distance to a *sit-stay*, for example, you are increasing the distance you step away from your dog while he is in the *sit-stay*. To set him up for success, you will take a step back in the exercise, and ask him to hold the *sit-stay* for a shorter period of time.

Time

Time is how long you ask a dog to maintain or hold a behavior. For example, when teaching the *stay* command, you will first ask

your pup to hold the *sit* or *down* for 5 seconds, and then praise and treat your puppy. When he is successful with that for multiple repetitions, you will ask him to hold it for 10 seconds, and so on. If he fails, then take the exercise back a step to an easier repetition, and build on that again.

PUTTING IT ALL TOGETHER

So, now you know the basics. It's all about taking small steps and building onto what the doodle already has mastered, one challenge or distraction at a time. When you add a challenge, make the task for the first few repetitions.

BASIC COMMANDS YOUR DOODLE NEEDS TO KNOW

If you teach your puppy only four commands, teach these basics: *sit, down, stay,* and *come.* Virtually every additional command and every sport will require knowing these basics. Even the youngest Labradoodle and Australian Labradoodle can learn these commands and be fluent in them before they are 4 months old.

Each of these four commands will follow the same training pattern of
- Shaping the behavior with a treat as a lure
- Rewarding the behavior with praise and a treat
- Repetition to cement the behavior
- Adding a verbal cue

Sit

The *sit* is a great all-purpose command that will keep your puppy from knocking the food bowl out of your hand, will keep your puppy calm when people want to pet him, and is a great "brake" when walking him and you need to regain his attention.

- **Shape the Sit:** Gently hold the puppy's collar in one hand and, with the other, hold the treat in your fingertips. Starting from the pup's nose, slowly move the treat from his nose to the top of his skull. Keep your hand barely above the puppy's head. At first, your pup will jump around a bit but then as he focuses, he will begin folding into a *sit*.
- **Reward Progress:** As your puppy starts rocking backward into a *sit*, it's okay to reward him for progress. Keep working to get him back into the *sit* and rewarding him as he makes more and more progress.
- **Repetition:** Keep working on your puppy's *sit* until he is regularly sitting as he follows the treat. When he is quickly and confidently sitting, then you can move to the next step.
- **Link the Verbal Command:** Start saying "*Sit!*" as he is sitting. Continue saying this as he sits (repetition).
- **Add Difficulty:** Begin to say "*Sit*" earlier in the luring phase. Praise and repeat until your doodle is sitting from a stand, when you say "*Sit!*" without using a lure.

Down

The *down* is a command that can be used to gently establish leadership. Additionally, the *down* can be helpful in preventing a dog from barking; it is very difficult to bark while in a *down*. It's also a great command to have in your puppy's arsenal for mealtimes—not his, yours.

- **Shape the Down:** While your puppy is in a *sit*, gently hold the puppy's collar in one hand, and with the other hold the treat in your fingertips, but this time move the treat from his nose backward into his chest and down. This is a tough move, but keep at it. Your puppy will most likely pop up to a stand and try to dip down with his front end and pop up his back end to get the treat. Be kind but persistent. Put him back in a *sit*, and then move the treat slowly again.
- **Reward Progress:** The *down* really takes a while for many puppies and adults to learn, so reward progress. Rewarding progress is one of the fastest ways to get him to eventually go into a *down*. Each time he makes

progress, reward him. But remember, he *does not* get a treat if he doesn't provide more effort and/or make progress toward the *down* position.

- **Repetition:** Once he finally understands that he is to lie fully down on the floor for the *down*, praise, treat, (celebrate a little!) and repeat. You want him hitting the floor as fast as possible before you add any extra challenges to this command.

- **Link the Verbal Command:** Link the command "*Down!*" only when your puppy is able to be lured completely to the *down* position on a regular basis and with speed and confidence. If he is at this point, link the verbal command "*Down!*" with the very final act of lying down. Praise, treat, and repeat.

- **Add Difficulty:** Start giving the command "*Down!*" when your puppy is two-thirds of the way into the *down*. Praise, treat, and

repeat. Continue backing up the verbal command until you can give the command and no longer use the treat to lure your doodle into a *down*.

Stay

The prerequisite to teaching this command is that your dog needs to be solid on his *sit* or his *down*. The *stay* command is technically adding the challenge of time to your doodle's *sit* or *down*. The *sit-stay* can be used when answering the front door to receive packages without having your doodle run out. The *sit-stay* can also be used for a more solid *sit* when introducing your doodle to people who can't have a dog jumping up on them. The *down-stay* is a perfect way to help a dog relax. Sounds odd, but if you work to have your doodle achieve a 20-minute *down-stay*, chances are he will become relaxed in that spot, too. The *down-stay* can be used during

Practical Commands to Learn, Too

Out or **Give** To teach this command, offer a high-priority treat to your doodle when he has a toy in his mouth or another item he is willing to trade for something yummy. As he drops the toy to take your treat, say the command, "*Out!*" or "*Give!*" Immediately give him the treat and give him back his toy. Repeat and treat whenever you have the opportunity.

Practical purposes: When your doodle has an item that he shouldn't have or one that he doesn't want to give up, the "*Out!*" command can be used, preventing the doodle from becoming injured or poisoned, or avoiding a confrontation with a doodle that might now want to give up a choice item.

Up and **Off** With a leash on your doodle, encourage him to jump up on a soft surface. If he's little, it can be as simple as a big pillow on the floor. If he's much bigger, it can be a low couch or even a bed. As he follows the treat onto the surface, say "*UP!*" and reward him. Using another treat, immediately lure him off the surface and say "*Off!*" as he jumps off. Reward and treat him, and tell him what a good boy he is!

Practical purposes: "*Up*" can be used to encourage doodles to jump into a van or the back of an SUV. "*Off*" can also be used to make a doodle get down from a couch, bed, or other position of what the dog sees as an authority position, without causing an ugly confrontation with a doodle who may want to be boss.

mealtimes (yours), and it can also be used as the basis for training a doodle to go to his spot, in which you will lure your puppy to a comfortable spot, marked with a specific pad or blanket, and put him in a *down-stay*. With patience and work, you will be able to tell him to "*Go to your spot,*" and your doodle will walk over to his bed and lie down.

The principles for the *stay* are the same whether it is for a *sit*, *down*, or *stand*. For this instruction, the *sit-stay* will be used.

- **Shape the *Sit-Stay*:** With the puppy in a *sit*—either next to you or in front of you—give him the hand signal and voice command for the *stay*. The hand signal, if you are in front of him, is holding your hand out, palm toward the doodle, fingers up. If you are next to your doodle, make sure he is on your left side and, using your left hand, move your hand in a short motion from right to left in front of your pup's nose, fingers down, and palm toward your puppy.

- **Reward Progress:** After saying "*Stay!*" *do not move.* Count to three and praise your puppy calmly, treat, and repeat.

- **Add Difficulty:** Increase the amount of time you make him *sit* by more seconds. Give the command with the hand signal, count, and then praise, treat, repeat. Increase the time so he is sitting for 30 seconds.

- **Change the Challenge**: Give your puppy the "*Stay!*" command, take one step away, and step immediately back. Praise, treat, repeat. When your puppy is solid on this, step away, hold for 5 seconds, and step back. Praise, treat, repeat. Continue to add either more time or more distance. BUT, if you increase time, reduce the distance at first. You are giving your puppy something you know he can accomplish. If you add distance, reduce the time away from the puppy.

- **Repetition:** Keep working on the length of time your doodle holds the *sit-stay* and slowly increase the distance between you and your doodle each time. This should always be practiced on leash. When you are ready to work farther than 6 feet from your puppy, invest in a longer leash or a recall or tracking leash so that you can work up to 30 feet away and still have a leash on your dog.

Come

The recall should be called the "life-saving" command. It's one you never hope to have to use off leash, but you want to practice this as much as possible to ensure that when you do call "*Come!*" your doodle stops what he is doing and runs to you.

- **Shape the Recall:** With your puppy on a leash, put him in a *sit-stay*, walk several steps away, turn and face your puppy. Say the command, "*Come!*" and start running backward, encouraging your puppy to come to you. Say the command only once, but give him a little tug on the leash to encourage him to break his *sit-stay.* Praise, treat, and repeat.
- Your puppy doesn't know a *sit-stay* yet? No problem. While you're walking your puppy on leash, suddenly start backing up. When your puppy turns to see what you're doing, encourage him to come toward you, saying

his name and cheering him on, but only say the command "*Come!*" as he runs to you. Praise, treat, and repeat!

- **Use Every Opportunity**: When do you know for a fact your doodle will come to you? Does he run to you when you are holding his dinner bowl? If you start running through the house, will he chase after you? Use these situations to help shape the *come.* In any instance, when he is running toward you and he is just about to crash into your legs, say, "*Come!*"
- **Repetition:** Keep working on your puppy's *recall* until every time you give him the command "*Come!*" he comes flying to you. But, no matter how good he gets, do not test his command skills off leash. It will only take one time when he does not come on command and is off leash (and plays the can't-catch-me game), and it will take months to train a reliable recall again.
- **Add Difficulty**: When your doodle is doing well on his *sit-stay* or *down-stay*, while making sure he is on a long leash, increase your distance away from him when you recall him. When you start adding new environments, reduce the distance away from your doodle and gradually build up to your previous distance but in the new environment.

WALK NICELY: TEACH THIS NOW

Teaching your doodle puppy to *walk nicely* next to you is something that can easily be taught when your puppy is little. He wants to follow you everywhere at this age and he is little, so if he goes in an opposite direction, he can easily be redirected. One way to increase

Heavy Pullers

If you have an older doodle who is dragging you, fit him with a training head collar, such as the Gentle Leader. This training tool will effectively turn your doodle around to face you every time he tries to lunge forward. Most older dogs learn to walk nicely with the head collar on. When you have control of your older doodle with the head collar, you can work on his walking nicely in a harness in quiet areas with few distractions at first. With any skill, repeat, praise good behavior, and treat.

your puppy's attentiveness is to tether him to you. Use a thin, lightweight leash that is 4 feet long, and clip one end to him and one end to your belt loop. While walking around, keep your puppy's attention and praise him for paying attention to you and staying close.

As your puppy gets older, it will be harder to keep his attention. You can carry a favorite toy and pull it out to play with him (a reward, too!). You can walk with treats. You can intersperse your walking with *sit* commands, changes of pace (take off running), and reverse directions frequently. Your neighbors may think you're crazy but don't worry—you'll have the best dog on the block soon.

Keep working with him. Walking nicely on a leash is going to be of utmost importance.

The first eight weeks of your puppy's socialization skills were up to the breeder; however, the rest of his life is up to you. Let's get started!

Making Introductions

Most happy, friendly Labradoodles and Australian Labradoodles will have no trouble making new friends. And his wiggles and kisses to people of all sizes, shapes, colors, and ages will be rewarded with attention and pats. The act of meeting people is self-rewarding: The puppy greets people, and he gets rewarded. Happy puppies can get so excited that they start jumping up on people. Jumping up is actually a friendly behavior, but it is a dog behavior and not appropriate when meeting people, especially little people. To curb his enthusiasm, without curbing his enthusiasm for meeting new people, try the following:

- Put the puppy in a *sit-stay.*
- Tell the person the puppy is only allowed to receive pats if he *sits.*
- Allow the person to pet the puppy.
- Ask the person if they would like to give the puppy a treat.
- Have the person give the puppy the "*Sit*" command.
- Let the person treat the puppy.

The Timid Doodle

If you have a shy doodle or one that is just lacking confidence, *do not force him to make introductions.* Socialization of the timid puppy is completely different from the outgoing puppy. It takes more time, more patience, and more attentiveness to the puppy's body language and comfort level.

- Allow the puppy to make the approach. If he wants to go meet someone, let him approach.
- If you detect any signs of fear (see "Body Language," below), exit the situation immediately.
- Allow the puppy to watch people from greater distances until you see he is exhibiting happy, loose body language.
- Give people treats and ask them to toss them to the puppy.
- If your puppy wants to meet the person, have him or her hold the treat in an open palm and allow the puppy to take it.
- Do not let people attempt to pat the puppy on the top of the head. Instead, ask them to scratch the pup under the chin.
- Keep building on positive experiences.

Body Language

If your dog is timid, it is very important to understand if your puppy needs to exit a situation (fear signs) or if he is making progress (friendly body language). It is equally important to know that intense fear triggers a flight or fight response. *Never put your doodle in a situation where he is so uncomfortable that he might make the fight response!* Yes, fear is the number one reason for dog bites. It outnumbers dominant aggression bites. So, know the signs.

Body Language of Fear: Lowered head; eyes looking up; not making eye contact and/or looking away; nervous panting; ears flattened against neck and pulled back; yawning; trembling; shaking; crouching; trying to run away; submissive urination; tucked tail (can be wagging and tucked); crying or whimpering; barking or silent; one paw raised (worried, not attempting to shake).

Note: fear can elevate to fear aggression.

Socializing with Other Dogs

When your puppy was with his litter-mates and his mother, he was receiving "doggie protocols" from his mother and the other puppies. Mothers will correct their pups if they are being overly mouthy or pushy. Littermates will react to "over-play" by crying out and refusing to play with the offending puppy. Most puppies learn how to behave around other pups in this manner. Once you've got your puppy, however, he doesn't have a lot of interaction with other dogs. A good solution to this is enrolling your puppy in a well-respected puppy kindergarten class. All pups will be of approximately the same age and the class should be divided by size, so that during the socialization part of the class (play), everyone is roughly equal.

In addition, the puppy kindergarten class will allow for play under the watchful eye of the lead trainer of the group, who will be able to show participants what good dog-to-dog interactions and body language are, and when a dog needs to be removed from a situation that could escalate into a bad experience.

Body Language of Dominant Aggression: Intense stare; locked eyes; piloerection (the raising of hair along a dog's neck and back); stiff, hard tail wag; ears forward; body straining forward; muscles taut; barking or mouth shut; low-range growling, or snarling; snapping; tail held high and stiff; posed to lunge.

Body Language of a Happy Dog: Relaxed body position; panting in a relaxed "smiling" expression; happy, relaxed ears—neither hard forward nor flattened on neck; enthusiastic, big, loose tail wag; tail thumping on floor; play bow (front end down, rear end up with tail wagging); overall impression of being soft and wiggly.

Information

USEFUL ADDRESSES AND CONTACTS

Organizations
Australian Labradoodle Association (ALA)
www.laa.org.au

Australian Labradoodle Association of
America (ALAA)
www.alaa-labradoodles.com

Australian Labradoodle Club of America
(ALCA)
www.australianlabradoodleclub.us

Activities
Agility
American Kennel Club (AKC)
www.akc.org

Canine Performance Events, Inc.
PO Box 80
South Lyon, MI 48178
www.k9cpe.com

North American Dog Agility Council
(NADAC)
24605 Dodds Road
Bend, OR 97701
www.nadac.com

United Kennel Club (UKC)
100 East Kilgore Road
Kalamazoo, MI 49002-5584
www.ukcdogs.com

United States Dog Agility Association
(USDAA)
PO Box 850955
Richardson, TX 75085-0955
www.usdaa.com

Canine Good Citizen
See "American Kennel Club" listing

Disc Dog
Ashley Whippet Invitational (AWI)
www.ashleywhippet.com

SkyHoundz
660 Hembree Parkway, Suite 110
Roswell, GA 30076
www.skyhoundz.com

Dock Jumping
DockDogs
www.dockdogs.com

See "United Kennel Club" Listing

Flyball
North American Flyball Association (NAFA)
1333 West Devon Avenue, #512
Chicago, IL 60660
www.flyball.org

Obedience
See "American Kennel Club" listing

See "United Kennel Club" listing

Rally
See "American Kennel Club" listing

See "United Kennel Club" listing

World Cynosport Rally
PO Box 850955
Richardson, TX 75085-0955
www.rallydogs.com

Therapy Dog
Pet Partners
875 124th Avenue NE, Suite 101
Bellevue, WA 98005
www.petpartners.org

Therapy Dog International (TDI)
88 Bartley Road
Flanders, NJ 07836
www.tdi-dog.org

Therapy Dogs United (TDU)
1932B West 8th Street
Erie, PA 16505
www.therapydogsunited.org

Health
DNA Testing
DDC® Veterinary
Animal DNA Testing
1 DDC Way
Fairfield, OH 45014

OptiGen®, LLC
Cornell Business & Technology Park
767 Warren Road, Suite 300
Ithaca, NY 14850
www.optigen.com

Paw Print Genetics
A division of Genetic Veterinary Sciences, Inc.
850 East Spokane Falls Boulevard, Suite 200
Spokane, WA 99202
www.pawprintgenetics.com

VetGen
Veterinary Genetics Services
3728 Plaza Drive, Suite 1
Ann Arbor, MI 48108
www.vetgen.com

Eye
Orthopedic Foundation for Animals (OFA)
Eye Certification Registry
2300 East Nifong Boulevard
Columbia, MO 65201-3806
www.ofa.org/eye_overview.html

American College of Veterinary
   Ophthalmologists®
PO Box 1311
Meridian, ID 83680
www.acvo.org

Elbows
See "Orthopedic Foundation for Animals"
   listing

Hips
Antech PennHip
Antech Imaging Services
17672-B Cowan Avenue
Irvine, CA 92614
www.pennhip.org

See "Orthopedic Foundation for Animals"
   listing

BOOKS

Dog Training

Arden, Andrea. *Dog Training Bible*. New York: Barron's Educational Series, 2011

Arrowsmith, Claire. *Instant Dog Training: The Quick Response Program*. New York: Barron's Educational Series, 2011

Arrowsmith, Claire. *The Sit Down Come Heel Stay and Stand Book*. New York: TFH Publications, Inc., 2008

McConnell, Patricia B. *The Puppy Primer*. McConnell Publishing, Ltd., 2nd Edition, 2010

Pelar, Colleen. *Puppy Training for Kids*. New York: Barron's Educational Series, 2012

Housetraining

McCullough, Susan. *Housetraining for Dummies, 2nd Edition*. New York: For Dummies, 2009

Socializing with Dogs

Bennett, Robin and Susan Briggs. *Off-leash Dog Play: A Complete Guide to Safety & Fun*. Iowa: RB Consulting, 1st Edition, 2008

Important Note

This pet owner's manual tells the reader how to buy or adopt, and care for, a Labradoodle or an Australian Labradoodle. The author and publisher consider it important to point out that the advice given in the book is meant primarily for normally developed dogs of excellent physical health and sound temperament.

Anyone who acquires a fully grown dog should be aware that the animal has already formed its basic impressions of human beings. The new owner should watch the animal carefully, including its behavior toward humans, and, whenever possible, should meet the previous owner.

Caution is further advised in the association of children with dogs, in meeting with other dogs, and in exercising the dog without a leash.

Even well-behaved and carefully supervised dogs sometimes do damage to someone else's property or cause accidents. It is therefore in the owner's interest to be adequately insured against such eventualities, and we strongly urge all dog owners to purchase a liability policy that covers their dog.

Index

About the Author

Joan Hustace Walker is the author of more than 20 pet books including *Barron's Dog Bible: Labrador Retrievers*. She has written hundreds of feature articles, has photographed hundreds of published images, and has received more than 30 national and international nominations and awards for her vast body of work.

A Note on Pronouns

Many dog lovers feel that the pronoun "it" is not appropriate when referring to a beloved pet. For this reason, Labradoodles are referred to as "he" throughout this book, unless the topic specifically relates to female dogs. No gender bias is intended by this writing style.

Photo Credits

iStock:
> Leppert: page 2
> LivingImages: page 29
> nallzchap: page 37
> NathanClifford: page 4
> PamelainBelfast: page 52
> sb rogan: pages 50, 58
> stockstudioX: page 23
> victoriarak: pages 43, 44

Shutterstock:
> Anna Hoychuk: page 24
> Annette Shaff: page 19
> Claudia Naerdemann: page 47
> Erik Lam: pages 8, 21, 67
> Gordo25: pages 34, 41, 54
> jadimages: page 72
> Jeanne Provost: page 89
> Joca de Jong: page 32
> John Wollwerth: page 66
> KariDesign: pages 3, 39, 61
> Marie Dolphin: page 71
> Mikkel Bigandt: page 18
> Peter Louwers: page 38
> Picture-Pets: pages 12, 15, 75
> rebeccaashworth: page 14
> Susan Harris: page 76
> The Dog Photographer: page 90
> Victoria Rak: pages 6, 11

Woof Tracks Photography: pages 16, 20, 26, 28, 30, 31, 33, 55, 56, 57, 63, 65, 78, 79, 82, 83, 84, 87

Cover Photos

Woof Tracks Photography: front cover (right center)
Shutterstock:
> Daz Stock: inside front cover
> jadimages: front cover (right bottom)
> Jeanne Provost: inside back cover
> Justin Sienkiewicz: front cover (right top)
> rebeccaashworth: back cover
> The Dog Photographer: front cover (left)

© Copyright 2017 by Barron's Educational Series, Inc.

All inquiries should be addressed to:
Barron's Educational Series, Inc.
250 Wireless Boulevard
Hauppauge, NY 11788
www.barronseduc.com

ISBN: 978-1-4380-0693-2

Library of Congress Control No.: 2016958671

Printed in China
9 8 7 6 5 4 3 2 1